· ANNIE PROULX'S

Brokeback Mountain and *Postcards*

MARK ASQUITH

continuum

Continuum

The Tower Building	80 Maiden Lane, Suite 704
11 York Road	New York
London SE1 7NX	NY 10038

www.continuumbooks.com

British Library Cataloguing-in-Publication Data
A catalogue record for this book is available from the British Library.

ISBN: 978-1-8470-6455-4 (Paperback)

Library of Congress Cataloging-in-Publication Data
A catalog record for this book is available from the Library of Congress.

Typeset by YHT Ltd
Printed and bound in Great Britain by the MPG Books Group

Contents

The Novelist

'Books speak even when they stand unopened on the shelf. If you would know a man or woman, look at their books, not their software.'

Annie Proulx, *New York Times*, 26 May 1994

Creating Proulx the novelist

Since E. Annie Proulx appeared on the literary stage with her collection of short stories *Heart Songs* (1988), she has cut a figure every bit as enigmatic as some of her fictional characters. Living most of her life in the country and enjoying rural pursuits, she has been portrayed, particularly by British critics, as a latter-day pioneer: in *The Times* Jason Cowley described her as a 'Pioneer poet of the American Wilderness', while David Thomson in the *Independent on Sunday* sought a Western cliché, describing her as 'The Lone Ranger' with 'dark, watchful eyes ... eyes to fit the Wyoming character, the former gunfighter who reckons on dying peaceably'. Proulx has rejected such labels as the product of 'commercialization' but nevertheless seems happy to cultivate such a persona. The photograph of the author that stares out from the dust-jacket of her novels establishes the element of choreographed authenticity that Proulx brings to the management of her image: it is both posed and natural – she is a rural woman and happy to project herself as such, bringing the same degree of care and attention to her creation of her literary persona as to her fictional characters. An early interview with David Streitfield in the *Washington Post*, for example, found her enumerating a catalogue of youthful adventures in a paragraph that would not have looked out of place at the beginning of one of her stories: 'Leaping a barbed wire fence and not making it; being grabbed on a lonely back lane by a strange older guy but biting and escaping; running away through the rain on the eve of a wedding ...'

To some extent, Proulx's most enduring character creation is her own persona, which emerges as the product of careful mediation between author, publisher and journalists. Like her characters, she appears in critical profiles as carved from the landscape; epithets such as 'gnarled', 'grizzled' and 'chiselled' punctuate descriptions of her face, while her eyes are invariably fixed as some point in the middle distance. Nicci Gerrard described her as a 'frontier woman' in an early review in the *Observer* – 'weather-worn, life-worn, as if she has spent years walking on hard earth against bitter winds'. In the *Independent* Ros Wynne-Jones made clear the fictional aspect in Proulx's presentation of herself by imagining her as an older character in one of her own stories: 'At 86, she had skin like a slipcover over a rump-sprung sofa, yet her muscled forearms and strong fingers suggested she could climb a sheer rock-face.' Complementing this hardy Western persona has grown the myth of Proulx the no-nonsense interviewee. One of her earliest profilers,

Katharine Viner of the *Guardian*, noted 'There is no other way to approach an interview with E. Annie Proulx except with fear ... she tells you if she finds your questions boring; she detests small talk.' David Thomson suggested worse, that to stray onto topics that she regarded personal was to be left 'leaning into the gunfighter's intransigence'. Aida Edemariam recorded just such a look when she asked a personal question during an early profile for the *Guardian*: 'her face hardens with a joke that's not quite a joke: "it's a good thing I put the guns away"'. To some extent all are playing a game which allows Proulx to perform a role while being deadly serious: the character she projects allows her to be evasive while conforming to the role of the rural writer who 'tells it as it is'. As fellow writer and Laramie neighbour Mark Jenkins has claimed, 'there is a part of her that's playing the character of the great American writer'. Part of that character is a brutal honesty.

Ironically, Proulx's most high-profile performance to date followed the 2006 Oscars in which Ang Lee's adaptation of *Brokeback Mountain* lost out to the film *Crash* in the category of Best Picture. Her response in the *Guardian*, menacingly entitled 'Blood on the Red Carpet', deliberately presents herself as a hick outsider and the voice of a mainstream American common sense, while simultaneously branding the LA metropolitan elite as 'conservative heffalumps' trapped in gated communities and deluxe rest-homes and dangerously out of touch with 'contemporary culture'. This is no mean feat when we consider that the subject of the film is rural homophobia and that it was condemned by the Middle America that she is seeking to represent, but Proulx pulls it off with the tone of gentle mockery and perceptive observation that we have come to admire in her work. (Exactly who is that man in the kilt who always appears at award ceremonies? she asks.) Her defiant closing statement both disarms her critics while carefully projecting her character: 'for those who call this little piece a Sour Grapes Rant, play it as it lays'.

Proulx's writing career

The biography available to the public is largely a composite of the various in-depth interviews with journalists, internet websites, and books such as Karen Rood's comprehensive study of the author's work, *Understanding Annie Proulx*, and Aliki Varvogli's excellent study of *The Shipping News*, which is part of this series. What follows is a résumé of her career to date, followed by an analysis of some of the major characteristics of her fiction.

E. Annie Proulx (the 'E' stands for Edna: she used her initial to get her stories published in hunting magazines but dropped it as 'it seemed more and more pompous') was born in Norwich, Connecticut in 1935, the eldest of five daughters, and grew up in New England and North Carolina. Rood notes that Proulx's father, George Napoleon Proulx, a French-Canadian immigrant, worked as a bobbin boy in a textile mill, eventually rising to become company vice-president. Her mother, Lois Gill, was an amateur naturalist and painter whose family had a 'strong tradition of oral storytelling' and whose painterly attention to detail taught Proulx to 'see'. As Proulx herself recollects: 'from the time I was extremely small, I was told, "look at that" ... from the wale of the corduroy to the broken button to the loose thread to the dishevelled moustache ...' Due to her father's work, Proulx attended a number of high schools in Vermont and North Carolina, and it is during these years that she cultivated her love of reading, choosing books initially by the colour of their dust-jackets before moving onto the novels of Jack London and Somerset Maugham, which she was reading by the tender age of seven. It is a habit that has remained with her throughout her life: 'I read omnivorously, I always have, my entire life. I would rather be dead than not read ...' Reading voraciously, she has argued, is the best way to learn to write, and yet she remains coy about literary influences, parrying questions with an evasive claim that they are too numerous to mention.

She entered Colby College in Waterville, Maine, in the class of 1957. Before graduating she dropped out to marry H. Ridgely Bullock, with whom she had one daughter, Sylvia Marion, who was brought up by her father upon their divorce in 1960. A second marriage soon afterwards produced two sons, Jonathan Edward and Gillis Crowell, but this too ended in divorce. In 1963 Proulx enrolled on a History BA at the University of Vermont, graduating in 1969; that same year she married James Hamilton Lang. Proulx had a third son, Morgan Hamilton, before this marriage also ended in divorce. Two of her marriages Proulx has described as 'terrible', noting, perhaps sardonically, that she has 'a talent for choosing the wrong people'.

After gaining an MA at Sir George Williams University (now Concordia University) in Montréal in 1973, Proulx enrolled for a PhD in Renaissance Economic History. Having passed the oral requirements, however, she was forced to leave her studies in order to look after her three sons. She moved to Canaan, on the US–Canada border, and was immediately faced with the problem of how to support a family while living in a remote rural retreat. She turned to freelance journalism, living in the woods like a latter-day Henry Thoreau producing 'How to ...' articles for local magazines on rural subjects such as cooking, fishing, hunting and gardening. It would be wrong, however, to characterize such articles as esoteric exercises in nostalgia for the urban market; rather they are part of Proulx's attempt to keep alive country traditions for future generations. As she explains: 'What interested me at this time was the back-to-the-land movement – communes, gardening, architecture ... observ[ing] what people were doing to make things work in rural situations'. Proulx made a good living for a number of years, dabbling with short stories on aspects of rural life 'for the intellectual stimulation' that she found fictional work provided. A number were published in *Gray's Sporting Journal*, and she recalls with fondness the 'intense camaraderie and shared literary excitement among the writers whose fiction appeared in Gray's, an experience without which, she maintains, she 'would probably never have tried to write fiction'.

Proulx's big break came in 1982 when, as Rood has observed, Tom Jenks accepted her story 'The Wer-Trout' for the June issue of *Esquire*. When he moved to take a job with the publishers Charles Scribner's Sons, he invited Proulx to collect some of her short stories together into a collection. The resulting *Heart Songs* (an old name for country and western music) was published in 1988. It focuses on the humdrum lives of the residents of Chopping County as they go about their daily routines of hunting, shooting and fishing. Beneath the veneer, however, she reveals a community brutalized by the harsh landscape and isolation, and a gallery of eccentric characters bearing ancient grudges, hidden secrets and under continual threat from outsiders – the kind of terrain that Proulx has been covering ever since. Critics were unanimous in heralding the arrival of a new and distinctive voice, characterized by its hard-bitten narrative tone, stacked metaphors and elliptical sentences that defied the rules of grammar. They also marvelled at the combination of gritty realism and surrealism. Tim Gautreaux in *The Boston Globe* placed Proulx in the same innovative category as Cormac McCarthy, claiming that behind the great stories 'there are great sentences' in which Proulx 'uses words the way a stonecutter uses his chisel'. Britain's *Sunday Times* heralded Proulx as 'America's most impressive new novelist', combining a 'tough knowledge-ableness' about rural lives 'with a style that is elatingly fresh and crisp with sensuous delicacy'.

Proulx's publishing contract with Scribner also asked for the publication of a novel, an idea that initially was met with incredulity by Proulx: 'I just laughed madly, had not a clue about writing a novel, or even the faintest desire. I thought of myself as a short story writer. Period, period, period.' Once she began, however, she was astonished at the speed of her adaptation: 'I sat down, and within a half-hour, the whole of *Postcards* was in my head,' and much to her surprise she relished not being restricted by a 5,000–6,000 word limit. Its critical success, of which more later, was immediate: the novelist Annie Proulx had well and truly arrived.

She was, however, troubled by criticism that *Postcards* was too dark and resolved to give her next novel, *The Shipping News*, a happy ending. As she somewhat mischievously recalls: 'A happy ending is wanted, is it? Let us see what we can do.' The setting is typical Proulx: a frozen Newfoundland fishing community threatened by over-fishing and government legislature, and her central character, Quoyle – a man with 'a great damp loaf of a body' and 'a head shaped like a Crenshaw' – falls woefully short of the heroic mould. And yet, after a catalogue of disasters recorded by an ambivalent narrator, including the loss of his job, parents, best friend and faithless wife, he is slowly healed in the landscape of his ancestors by an aunt who carries her own burden of an abused childhood. Eventually he finds 'happiness' in marriage to a local woman, but here, as Proulx cynically observes, 'happiness is simply the absence of pain, and so, the illusion of pleasure'. It worked: gone were some of the stylistic excesses of *Postcards*, and with a more linear narrative and more accessible prose the book became an instant bestseller; it won the Pulitzer Prize and was made into a film in 2002 with Kevin Spacey playing the lead. Proulx was happy with the results, claiming that 'they did a good job of it'.

The success of *The Shipping News* projected Proulx into the limelight, a place where she has seldom felt comfortable. She abhors celebrity, condemning a 'meat-rack kind of sensation' in which you are fêted as a prize winner by people who 'don't particularly care about your writing or what you're trying to say'. More practically, she hates the way that it impinges on her writing time. Proulx is at her happiest among her research papers: She rises around 4 a.m., writes in longhand (she believes the computer produces facile prose), and types up in the afternoon. In her rather cruelly titled 1997 profile, 'Happier to Write than Love', the British journalist Ros Wynne-Jones noted of the writing process: 'Prose pours out at a furious pace, often without time-consuming prepositions, as if she is on a pay-phone and has only 10 pence in which to say it all.' She intersperses writing-time with hikes in the country as, she maintains, she is 'able to untangle characters and plot lines and so forth more easily when walking'. She claims never to have suffered from writer's block; novels work themselves out in her head so that 'each one is like a wrapped package' awaiting transference to paper. It is, however, this process of transference that she found compromised by her celebrity status, leading her to wonder whether she would ever have time to write again.

It is ironic, therefore, that her next novel, *Accordion Crimes* (1996), proved to be her longest and most intricately plotted to date. Christina Patterson noted in the *Observer*: 'America is both the subject and the theme of this hugely ambitious work, which explores the pursuit of the American Dream through countless generations of immigrants.' The narrative, to some extent, blurs the distinction between novel and short story because there are eight separate sections, each containing a cast of new characters embroiled in a variety of different stories. The only link between them is a green accordion, which passes from generation to generation. Her most overtly political novel, it catalogues the exploitation of generations of immigrant labourers as they land in search of the American Dream; but it is also about the loss of cultural identity – language, names and music – that comes as a part of assimilation. Once again, the novel was well reviewed, though some were troubled by the novel's violence, a criticism that Proulx rejects, arguing: 'America is a violent, gun-handling country.' The reviewer for the *Glasgow Herald*, like so many others, was captivated by the novel's ambitious scale: 'It is impossible not to be overawed by the continuous invention, the panoramic range of achievement.'

The novel was nominated for an Orange Prize, but didn't win, possibly because of Proulx's reaction when she found out that it was for women's writing: 'How I hate that ... collections of women writers. How disgusting! They're writers, period. Yikes!' Proulx expanded this antipathy in an essay entitled 'Tell it Like a Person' published in the *Observer* in 1997. In it she denied the validity of the crude category of 'women's writing', arguing that gender issues do not inform technique, and that the old binary relationship of male/female experience (which she argues was always closer than has been accepted) has been broken down by the onset of the information age, which has 'made us aware of the complexities of categories, the infinite possibilities of sub-heads and cross-indexing'. She also takes issue with feminist critics who have criticized her for writing almost exclusively, and convincingly, from the male point of view and not engaging sufficiently with the female experience. Her argument, that in the rural communities in which her stories are set women are confined to domestic duties while 'men are outside doing the interesting things', can hardly have assuaged feminist concerns, while her mischievous assertion that, having grown up in a female household, 'men are very interesting to me', seems deliberately provocative.

In 1995 Proulx moved to Wyoming, a region to which she had taken a fancy during the research for *Postcards*, and one which informed her new short story collection *Close Range: Wyoming Stories*. Proulx's return to the short story format can be explained by her belief that a short story collection is the best way for a writer to illustrate a particular period or place because it is like taking 'the reader inside a house of windows, each opening onto different but related views – a kind of flip book of place, time and manners'. It is also clear that after such a long novel she found the brevity of the form a welcome change, since the need for compression offers a different set of challenges. 'There's no room for error in short stories,' she maintains; 'the lack of a comma can throw everything off.' This council of perfection leads her to revise her drafts as many as 30 or 40 times. The results of such care are breathtaking; Proulx's windows open on a world inhabited by characters as tough as beef jerky, whose catalogue of rape, infanticide, serial murder, paedophilia and genital mutilation is dismissed with the folksy explanation: 'When you live a long way out you make your own fun.'

Close Range was followed three years later by another novel, *That Old Ace in the Hole* (2002), which took Proulx to the fictional Woolybucket in the Texas and Oklahoma panhandles and a ranching community threatened by corporate hog-farming operations. Like *Accordion Crimes*, the novel blurs genre boundaries; Caroline Moore of the *Spectator* notes that it is really 'more a series of short stories than a novel', in which the passive central character, the luckless Bob Dollar, acts as the outsider (much like Quoyle in *The Shipping News*) to whom a cast of eccentrics relate their stories. And what tales they are, revealing Proulx's familiar preoccupation with murder, incest and a spirited defence of the Ku Klux Klan by the members of the ladies sewing circle. Others are more informative, sometimes verging on didacticism. The story of how the landscape was tamed by a Dutch windmill engineer (he was to have been the central character but Proulx's frustration at not being able to attend a course in the art of windmill engineering at Los Curces, New Mexico, led to the point of view shifting), provides a valuable insight into the way the environment was moulded, though it is seldom engaging. This, most critics argued, was the novel's greatest weakness. For once, the alchemical mix of fact and fiction had not quite worked, Laura Miller complaining in the *New York Times* that 'she has collected quite a pile of stuff – history, economics, folkways and local lore – to shoehorn into this novel, and the result is decidedly lumpy'. It is a weakness that Proulx herself acknowledges: 'for this book I did too much, really, and have boxes and boxes of material I could not use'. Indeed, she was so exhausted by the research that she told the British journalist Aida Edemariam that she would never write another novel.

Instead she turned to short stories, publishing a companion collection to *Close Range*, *Bad Dirt* in 2004. Whereas the former chronicled the plight of characters shaped by the oppressive Wyoming landscape, this collection focuses on its incomers, both the urban rich and trailer-park rednecks. The tone is lighter, and characters, who in *Close Range* were grotesque eccentrics with sinister buried secrets, have been transformed into burlesques engaging in slapstick antics such as beard-growing contests and transforming cooking cauldrons into hot tubs. For the critic John Harrison, writing in *The Times Literary Supplement*, there is a failure of art in Proulx's characterization, and whereas in *Close Range* they 'seemed to spring from the plains like some kind of vegetation', in *Bad Dirt* they seem to have emerged 'from the archives of the McKracken Research Library'. Black comedy has been transformed into screwball, leading Terence Rafferty to argue in the *New York Times*: 'When you look at the West and all you can see are the wide-open spaces between people's ears, it's time to hit the trail.'

Proulx hasn't forsaken the West: the title of her third collection of Wyoming Stories, *Fine Just the Way It Is* (2008), offers an unconscious riposte to those critics who have suggested that the landscape is written out. Indeed, Marcela Valdes argues in the *Washington Post* that the collection 'excavates new riches from [the] golden vein' of 'casually brutal stories' with which she has dazzled the reader for the past three decades. For most critics the collection marked a return to form for Proulx, many offering comparisons between the emotional trajectory, narrative control and elegiac power of the stories, particularly the unfortunately titled 'Tits up in a Ditch', and what still remains her most famous story, *Brokeback Mountain*. Gone are the comic excesses of *Bad Dirt*, and in their place Proulx offers vividly evoked characters trapped in dramas of endurance set against the unforgiving landscape. It is a collection that proves, according to Stephen Abell writing in *The Times Literary Supplement*, 'that them old cowboy songs of struggle and loss' are still relevant and emotionally powerful, and that there is no better storyteller than Proulx, whose 'writing can be as fine as anything being produced in America today'.

Her latest project, *Red Desert: History of a Place* (2008), takes her away from fiction back to her roots in history. What started as an introductory essay to a collection of photographs by Martin Stupich rapidly mushroomed into a collection of essays by scientists and historians on a disappearing landscape, that of Wyoming's Red

Desert. The work is neither a sanctimonious plea to save the environment – she despairs at the impotence of the environmental lobby – nor a glossy coffee table book: it is, Proulx insists, a commemoration of a dying landscape. However, despite the book's insistent regionalism, Proulx argues that the plight of the Red Desert is emblematic of many global landscapes threatened by corporate greed and global warming. The book, she hopes, will act as a catalyst for action, propelling naturalists, historians, geologists and the everyday residents of Wyoming to visit and take note of the 'beauty of what remains in this little known place', and act on what they see for the good of the planet.

The characteristics of Proulx's fiction

First published at the age of 57, Proulx does not regret her belated arrival as a fiction writer. She employs a typically Proulx-like metaphor to explain that it is 'important to know how the water's gone over the dam before you start to describe it. It helps to have been over the dam yourself.' Her meaning here extends to emotional empathy rather than the subject matter of her books, for when it comes to the latter she rejects the advice given to young authors to 'write about what you know' because she believes that it produces 'nothing but interior self-examination'. Successful writing, for Proulx, is a combination of experience and curiosity – if we continue to swim in the same water, 'we never grow. We don't develop any facility for languages, or an interest in others, or a desire to travel and explore and face experience head-on.' Put like this, it's better to shoot the dam!

Her fiction begins with landscape. 'For me,' she told the *Guardian*'s Aida Edemorian 'the story falls out of a place, its geology

and climate, the flora, fauna, prevailing winds, the weather.'
(Sentiments amplified in her essay 'Dangerous Ground: Landscape
in American Fiction', 2003.) And what climate and landscape it is,
battering those characters who try to scrape a living from its
margins. This approach to her environment is clearly influenced by
Canadian literature, or, at least, by Margaret Atwood's classic work
Survival: A Thematic Guide to Canadian Literature (1972), a work that
would have been very hard to avoid for a postgraduate student in
Montréal in 1973. Atwood, and others, like Northrop Frye, point
out that the Canadian response to the landscape – viewing it as
harsh and menacing – is different from the typical American attitude, in which Nature was, until recently, characterized as idyllic.
It is these brutal landscapes that are central to Proulx's work,
distinguishing her from those contemporary 'regional' writers who
employ landscape to add authenticity and 'local colour' to their
narratives.

The closest contemporary writer is Cormac McCarthy, with
whom she shares, as Joyce Carol Oates has noted, an 'aesthetic
wonderment for the physical terrain of the West and the big skies
above', which borders on reverence, combined with a horror at the
brutality of the lives of those forced to live in it. But whereas
McCarthy's tone of Biblical declamation continually dignifies the
suffering of his characters, raising it to a level commensurate to the
landscape, Proulx is more interested in the incongruity between
the sublime environment and the difficult lives of ordinary people.
This largely comes from her training as a historian, particularly her
interest in the historical methodology of the French *Annales* School
during her time as a PhD student. Popular in the first half of the
twentieth century, it deliberately rejected history as a linear record
of the lives of 'great people' and focused instead on the ordinary
and marginalized (the farmers, ploughmen, etc.) set against the

power of the environment – geographical, economic and social. The historian of a given period, therefore, should begin by exploring the way in which the landscape and climate shaped the lives of its inhabitants before, as Proulx herself has noted, moving onto a 'minute examination of the lives of ordinary people through account books, wills, marriage and death records, farming and craft techniques'.

In many ways Proulx sees herself as the 'historian' of regions and ways of life that are under threat: 'I try to define periods when regional society and culture, rooted in location and natural resources, start to experience the erosion of traditional ways, and attempt to master contemporary, large-world values.' Her starting point is not the communities themselves but the primeval land-scape underpinning transient human activity. As Proulx herself has observed, 'I long ago fell into the habit of seeing the world in terms of shifting circumstances overlaid upon natural surroundings', so getting the bedrock right is of primary importance. We are con-stantly reminded in Proulx's fiction that where cattle now graze dinosaurs once roamed, and that where ranches now stand the sea once lapped. Her characters grow out of their environment; the character of Perley in the aptly entitled short story 'Bedrock' (*Heart Songs*) emerges from and is nurtured by the rock beneath his farm: 'atoms of this granite whirled in his body. Its stony, obdurate qualities passed up through the soil and into plant roots. Whenever he took potatoes from the heat-cracked bowl, his bones were hardened, his blood fortified' (p. 44). Elsewhere, her characters emerge from their primordial surroundings – their fists like rocks, fingers like carrots and hair like bunch grass – and face such his-torical magnitude with indifference. It is only the outsiders who, by reason of their detachment, seem conscious of the power exerted by the land. When, for example, the urbanite Mitchell Fair arrives in Wyoming we are told that 'he felt as though he had stumbled into a landscape never before seen on the earth and at the same time that he had been transported to the Ur-landscape before human beginnings' ('Man Crawling out of Trees', *Bad Dirt*, p. 106).

Welcome to Proulx country – although readily locatable on a map, it is a landscape made fantastic by the immensity of its history and its oppressive influence upon those who scratch a living from its soil.

Having established the bedrock, Proulx then, in *Annales* fashion, immerses herself in the local community. She carries a sleeping bag in the back of her truck, hires a shack or erects a tent and 'hangs out' while she tries to fix its distinct identity – the rhythms of its speech, its gossip and preoccupations, its relationship with the broader environment. She engages in archival research – reading local newspapers, dictionaries of slang, regional weather reports, botanists' plant guides – and carries out interviews with experts on subjects ranging from boat building to trapping, all of whom she acknowledges at the beginning of her novels, a practice more commonly associated with academic works. Indeed, the Acknowledgements page signals Proulx's historical ambitions in her work, the British reviewer Ruth Scurr perceptively noting that 'there is a serious and comprehensive aspiration to know a place, a project of understanding reminiscent of Alexis de Tocqueville's *Democracy in America*'.

This detailed research lends Proulx's fiction its verisimilitude: when a sandwich is made we know what knife is used and the order in which the ingredients are layered, and when a character speaks the dialogue is convincing. However, during the writing process, Proulx the historian gives way to Proulx the writer, and the tales overheard in the barroom are subject to the operation of the imagination. Some idea of the alchemy that takes place during those early morning writing sessions can be gleaned through her treatment of her characters. Their names may be culled from local directories, but they are far from composites of all those hours spent in the library. There is the slovenly, alcoholic Car Scrope, 'held together with dozens of steel pins, metal plates, and lag screws', who presides over the downfall of the Coffeepot Ranch ('A Pair of Spurs', *Close Range*); Sherriff Hugh Dough, a 40-year-old bed-wetter with 'black eyes like those in a taxidermist's draws' who has an incestuous relationship with his sister (*That Old Ace in the Hole*); or Ottaline Touhey, 'the size of a hundred-gallon propane tank', who is so lonely that she strikes up a relationship with the wreck of her father's John Deere tractor ('The Bunchgrass Edge of the World', *Close Range*). The point seems to be that, in Proulx's world, extreme landscapes combine with loneliness and boredom to reduce human beings to their base elements, a mixture of inbreeding, petty squabbles, insatiable libido and fragile impotence. Thus, as her narratives deftly navigate their way between the tragic and darkly comic, she offers the reader a gallery of grotesques lurching towards the caricature.

Proulx's characterization has many literary antecedents, Dickens being an obvious precursor, but a perhaps more significant forerunner is Sherwood Anderson, whose *Winesburg, Ohio* (1919) was an experimental project which sought, like Proulx's, to combine the short story and the novel by allowing characters to drift in and out of each of the 26 tales. Through his 'grotesques' Anderson explores the way in which character is distorted through alienation, loneliness and, above all, a loveless marriage. Wash Williams and Wing Biddlebaum are both creations worthy of Proulx. The first is an obese and filthy misogynist who, as the local telegraph operator, is responsible, ironically, for connecting people; the second is a sensitive ex-schoolteacher accused of molesting a male pupil, an outcast who has difficulty controlling his sensitive, roaming hands. However, whereas Anderson is interested in the interior lives of his characters, carefully picking over their emotional biographies, hopes and delusions, for the illumination and entertainment of the reader, Proulx is clear in her rejection of the psychological novel: 'I do not attempt the interior novel ... I always place my characters against the idea of *mass*, whether landscape or a crushing social situation or powerful circumstances.' Her subject may be small-town but her scope is epic, placing her in an older tradition of 'naturalist writers', such as Emile Zola, Thomas Hardy and John Steinbeck, for whom external influences (such as landscape and economic forces) and internal forces (such as the uncontrollable power of lust or ambition) proved a massive presence dictating the subject, content and plot of their works.

Proulx's epical ambitions mean that her novels, and even her short stories, often cover several generations. 'I tend to look at the long span of life, not just episodes,' she has remarked, a timescale which enables her to chart fully the detrimental effect of the forces acting upon her characters. Furthermore, because she is frequently attempting to capture the wholesale decline of a region, her novels generally contain a large number of characters. Some, of course, appear fleetingly; offering regional colour or evidence of a particular point of view or theme, but however brief their appearance, Proulx's skilful biographical compression means that their presence is fully realized. For example, in *Postcards* the insurance assessor Vic Bake is introduced with 'a face like a scoop of mashed potato ... incorruptible, a tattletale in youth, a teacher's pet, a winner of gold stars, he was now trying for a bigger role' – the simile emphasizing his pale, pasty features (a contrast to the good-hearted ruddy complexions of the others in the office), while the biography captures the uneasy combination of ruthlessness and moral righteousness (p. 120). Even major characters can be subject to the same compression, the narrative selection of those aspects of their lives worthy of development providing an interesting study in itself. The opening paragraph of *The Shipping News* provides an excellent example, as here the grand panorama of the first 36 years of Quoyle's life is reduced to just over a hundred words. Significantly, the narrator actively draws attention to this act of compression in an off-hand opening sentence, which successfully establishes the indifferent narrative tone that will dominate the text while also accentuating the weakness of the central character (a quality symbolized through the 'quoyle' of rope – which, we are told, 'can be walked on if necessary' – that heads the chapter):

Here is an account of a few years in the life of Quoyle, born in Brooklyn and raised in a shuffle of dreary upstate towns.

Hive-spangled, gut roaring with gas and cramp, he survived childhood; at the state university, hand clapped over his chin, he camouflaged torment with smiles and silence. Stumbled through his twenties and into his thirties learning to separate his feelings from his life, counting on nothing. He ate prodigiously, liked a ham knuckle, buttered spuds.

The mutilated sentences, which lack pronouns – reflecting the invisibility of Quoyle himself – offer an economical impression rather than a developed character. And his temperament is captured: his homely appetites, his physical and social awkwardness, his irritating, ingratiating passivity.

The compressed sentence has become Proulx's trademark, its amputated, elliptical phrases combining to defy normal grammatical conventions in an effort to capture the essence of both character and environment. Also central to the success of such writing has been the incorporation of the stacked metaphor, often two or three in a row, through which Proulx creates linguistic echoes which develop a sense beyond the denotative meaning of the words in isolation. For many critics, this aspect of Proulx's writing has given to her prose a poetic quality. Stephen Abell, for one, called his review of *Fine Just the Way It Is* in *The Times Literary Supplement* 'Annie Proulx's Prairie Poetry' and demonstrated how her stacked metaphors meld character with their environment. In 'Them Old Cowboy Songs', for example, the agony of Rose McLaverty as she experiences a stillbirth is reflected in her surroundings: 'The twitching bed leg, a dank clout swooning over the edge of the dishpan, the wall itself bulging forward ... all pulsing with the rhythm of her hot pumping blood.' The metaphors, Abell notes, are 'travesties of images of love and life' – the twitching infant corpse, 'the swoon of affection, the bulge of pregnancy, the pulse of the heart' – evidence of the shared harshness of landscape and human lives. John Skow's review of *Close Range* for *Time Magazine* is also interesting for his focus on the poetic quality of Proulx's language. Quoting the opening sentence of 'The Half Skinned Deer' – 'In the long unfurling of his life, from tight-wound kid hustler in a wool suit riding the train out of Cheyenne to geriatric limper in this spooled-out year, Mero had kicked down thoughts of the place where he began, a so-called ranch on strange ground at the south hinge of the Big Horns' – he offers the following interpretation: 'this is a remarkable sentence ... "Spooled-out year" and "kicked down" suggest a man who tossed his mental baggage together in a hurry, and "strange ground" says something of where he is going. As always, when signs are this clear that an author knows her trade, the reader signs on for the journey.'

Not all critics have been as eager to sign up for the ride. B. R.

Myers, for one, argues in his article 'A Reader's Manifesto: An attack on the growing pretentiousness of American literary prose', published in the *Atlantic Monthly* in 2001, that it has become fashionable for novelists 'to exploit the licence of poetry while claiming exemption from poetry's rigorous standards of precision and polish'. Proulx's metaphor pile-ups, he argues, are a case in point: they are designed to be read quickly, beguiling the reader with a pyrotechnic display of word play; but when considered more carefully, they prove to be lazy and inconsistent and, as a result, far from giving rural workers a voice, they simply divorce form from content. Taking issue with Skow's analysis, he argues that Proulx's apparent intention of a unified conceit simply does not work: '*unfurling*, or spreading out, as of a flag or an umbrella, clashes disastrously with the images of thread that follow. (Maybe "unravelling" didn't sound fancy enough.) A life is *unfurled*, a hustler is *wound tight*, a year is *spooled out*, and still the metaphors continue, with *kicked down* – which might work in less crowded surroundings, though I doubt it – and *hinge*, which is cute if you've never seen a hinge or a map of the Big Horns.'

The literary establishment relishes this sort of spat; it takes writers from the review sections to opinion columns. Jonathan Yardley of the *Washington Post* could hardly contain his glee with Myers' broadside, laying the blame for the 'writerly prose' to which Myers alludes, on creative writing courses which diminish the importance of plot, narrative and character, in favour of a form of narcissism in which the writer gazes adoringly at himself while claiming 'I'm a writer.' More than anything else, the disagreement highlights just how slippery the notion of good writing is – a fact that should give pause for thought as we formulate our own responses to Proulx's fiction.

What follows is a study of her first novel, *Postcards*, and the short story *Brokeback Mountain*, works showing Proulx at the height of her powers in different prose genres. Both explore the kind of themes that preoccupy Proulx's fiction: the buried sexual secret that eats at the heart of the protagonists; man's relationship with both the landscape and society; the breakdown of rural communities; and the marginalization of women. Both centre on tough 'cowboys' who express themselves through action and who find articulating feelings difficult. Her scope is epic, each tale narrated through a series of fragmentary snapshots by a third-person narrator, whose tobacco-spitting tone resembles that of the central characters. Proulx elevates each to the level of tragedy, her protagonists struggling against forces, internal and external, explored through a typology drawn from Classical and Biblical symbolism. *Postcards* is of particular interest because it shows an early Proulx willing to experiment with innovative narrative techniques and push grammar and syntax to its breaking point. *Brokeback Mountain* reveals a more restrained writer, but a more accomplished storyteller.

2

The Novel: *Postcards*

Stylistic features

Postcards is a novel about change, adaptation and survival, its epigraph highlighting the need for people to adjust themselves 'to beams falling' and then, when 'no more of them fell', to alter in accordance with this new reality. A farm brought to the brink of extinction by a blinkered patriarch, an accidental murder, a lost arm, a lost child – the beams fall hard and fast in the novel, punishing her isolated characters with Biblical vehemence. The landscape is unyielding, transforming domestic tribulations into epical feats of endurance. And yet her tone is never so elevated that we are unable to see the characters in front of us; the time spent listening to gossip, stories and advice on fur-trapping has not been wasted. Nor has the time spent in the local library sifting through innumerable documents, during which time she stumbled upon a collection of Vermont fire marshal's reports from the 1930s that, she recalls, included 'a number of dismal accounts of farmers burning down their houses and barns for the meagre insurance money' – the inspiration behind a key moment in her narrative. The character Loyal Blood, she remembers, 'leaped complete and whole formed from a 1930s Vermont state prison mug shot' on one of 'a small stack of postcards sent out by the Windsor Prison warden's office'. She kept the collection, showing them to Patti Doten of *The Boston Globe* just after the novel's publication and urging her: 'Look at the desolate and disturbing looks on their faces. They are finished faces. They are faces with no chances' – Loyal's face. It is the 'postcards', she claims, 'that started me writing my book', offering both inspiration for her central protagonist and an effective organizational device within the novel's narrative framework.

Despite such local detail, Proulx's scope remains epic, placing her in the company of naturalist writers such as Steinbeck, another chronicler of the rural dispossessed, and Frank Norris, whose most notable work, *McTeague* (1898), offers an interesting literary antecedent. Norris was preoccupied by social Darwinism, particularly how the civilized man must struggle with his animalistic tendencies, both violent and sexual. He explored this theme in *McTeague*; the eponymous anti-hero kills his wife and triggers a chain of events which in turn release underlying forces. Such concerns are, of course, central to the plot of *Postcards*: Loyal's crime is, to some extent, the product of his inherited blood, against which he must struggle. Norris is also interesting to Proulx aesthetically, for in his *The Responsibilities of the Novelist* (1903) he rejected the novel as social reportage and also the ascendancy of the linear narrative form in favour of a panorama displaying the struggles of ordinary people through a fragmentary observed experience. His ideas, heavily influenced by the French Impressionist movement and the work of the French Naturalist writer Emile Zola, found their clearest expression in John Dos Passos's USA trilogy (*The 42nd Parallel* (1930), *1919* (1932), *The Big Money* (1936)). Like *Accordion Crimes*, Dos Passos offers a history of the United States through the plight of marginalized immigrant labourers. He does not give a linear history, nor is there a central character or single story. Rather, he dips in and out of the stories of various immigrant groups, punctuating the narrative with 'Newsreel' and 'Camera Eye' sections. These techniques, borrowed from the early days of film, are designed to challenge the authority of a single narrative voice and immerse the reader in the information chaos experienced by his characters.

In many ways *Postcards* offers an updated version of Norris's vision, in which the wholesale decline of American society is reflected through the demise of a single community over a number of years. In the novel, Proulx eschews a linear narrative in favour of a series of fragments held together by a strong third-person narrator who zooms in and out of the action while drifting between the subjective experiences of different characters. For example, the staleness of Mernelle's marriage to Ray MacWay is communicated to the reader less through narrative comment than the carefully observed details of her vulgar living room furniture and the oppressive pleasantries of a shared evening meal (pp. 244–5). Similarly, we learn little of Dub's struggle to become a millionaire; we are simply presented with two contrasting images of him as a student of the motivational speaker, Maurice Bent, and as the linen-suited businessman in his own tropical paradise (pp. 163, 273). The reader is forced to fill in the void, meaning, as Proulx has noted, that 'the reader writes most of the story'.

There is nothing unusual in this, since this is what fiction writers do, but in Proulx's work this literary fragmentation is taken to extremes. There is an extreme elasticity in her narrative focus:

Loyal's travels as a uranium prospector, 'ROAMING OVER THE DUSTY Colorado Plateau, following the Morrison formation to Utah's Uinta range, to Wyoming into the Great Divide basin and up to the Gas Hills ...' receive less page space than Mrs Big Pinetree's preparation of a chicken sandwich (pp. 165, 30). The effect of this bewildering telescoping of action is that the reader is continually kept in a state of disequilibrium: he is invited to write parts of the story himself, and then co-opted into an extremely tightly controlled narrative frame, often with wider implications. This effect is supplemented by Proulx's incorporation of a number of innovative stylistic techniques which place further inter-pretative demands on the reader. The 'What I see' chapters, which will be discussed in detail in the section 'What the wanderer sees', are modelled on Dos Passos's 'Camera Eye' sections, and offer the reader an opportunity to experience, with the present tense immediacy of a fragmentary stream of consciousness, the unme-diated reaction to scenes observed by various characters through the car windscreen, or from the washing line. The postcards themselves offer even more interpretative potential, particularly because we are not the intended recipient. We are constantly being encouraged to snoop on half-disclosed secrets, and work out the rest for ourselves in an act of literary detection: a fascinating task, worthy of careful consideration.

The postcards of Postcards

Each chapter (and here it is tempting to think in terms of 'frag-ment' since the former suggests a degree of coordination that the text continually compromises) is headed by a title – which is often oblique in meaning – and a postcard (sometimes hardly legible), which seemingly bears little relation to it. In general terms, they add to the novel's sense of verisimilitude, their scruffy handwritten presentation suggesting that these are genuine artefacts written by real people with lives outside the focus of the narrative. Furthermore, because most of them are dated and appear chronologically, they perform an organizational function throughout the novel's broad sweep. It is, however, during the process of reading that their true function becomes apparent as we are invited to make connections between the postcard, the chapter title and the text.

Broadly speaking, the postcards fall into two categories. First of all, some act as catalysts setting in motion the events of the chapter, while filling in certain plot details; second, others are clearly written after the events of the chapter have taken place and to some extent pre-empt the contents while offering oblique, sometimes coldly objective summaries which transform our reading experience. Of the first variety, the chapter 'The Troubles of Celestial Bodies' is prefaced by Loyal's application for the job of building assistant (p. 190); his departure is caused by the anonymous allegations made in the postcard prefacing 'Obregón's Arm' (p. 207). Similarly, 'The Weeping Water Farm Insurance Office' is prefaced by Mink's insurance claim (p. 118); and the chapter in which Jewell begins the drive to her death is prefaced by mail-shot advertising a car for sale (p. 237). An example of a postcard of the second variety is that which prefaces the chapter 'Pala', in which the reader learns that she will become Dub's wife before the interview in which he is introduced to her, thus placing the reader in a privileged position from which he can observe any signs of affection breaking through the businesslike formality (p. 205). Conversely, we learn of the murderous brutality of Kortnegger (the farmer who briefly employs Loyal later in the novel), through an accusatory postcard penned by Loyal to the chief of police in Idaho before we actually meet him, which means that when reading we fear for all who come into contact with him, including his wife (p. 313). Finally, 'Down in the Mary Mugg' is prefaced by a postcard recommending that the victims of a mine disaster would make a good hypothermia study, a feature which highlights the increasing ambivalence of large economic and academic institutions to human suffering, a theme that will recur throughout the text (p. 91).

There is also a further grouping of unsolicited printed postcards which serve to draw out ironic parallels between the plights of the central characters. Dub and Loyal, for example, both receive cards confirming appointments – the first shows that the IRS are chasing Dub for tax irregularities, the second that the doctors are chasing Loyal because he is dying of a lung disease – which ends up, ironically, in the 'Dead Letter Office' (pp. 288, 301). The novel begins and ends with two unsolicited mail-shots: the first attempts to sell an electric fence to enclose Loyal's pasture, the second is a free flight offer from a travel agency run by Pala, offering Kevin Witkin, who is living on Loyal's pasture, the chance to escape his messed up life (pp. 3, 336). Thus the novel's central irony is laid bare: the 'short, sharp shock' will not be administered by electrification (which would help save the farm), but by Loyal's rape of Billy and subsequent flight, a crime that will be repeated years later on the same ground by Kevin Witkin (of which more later). The narrator is also interested in those responsible for such mail-shots, men like Loyal's childhood companion, Ronnie Nipple, whose foray into real estate begins with a folksy mail-shot which uses the neighbourly postcard as a business tool (p. 78). The attitude of the narrator is made clear by the title prefacing this chapter, which focuses on the distance between illusion and reality: 'Tickweed' is a beautiful flower that hides a parasitical weed, an apt symbol for the smooth-tongued Ronnie.

Tom Shone, reviewing the novel in *The Sunday Times*, argued that Proulx had reinvigorated the epistolary novel, adding that 'postcards have one advantage over letters for the novelist: the added pathos of private matters half-glimpsed by prying eyes, there for all to read'. Not only are we not the intended recipient, but we only have one side of the communication, from which we are invited to form judgements on both writer and addressee. The history of the Blood family is captured in their postcards, mostly in their slips and evasions. Loyal, for example, continues to mail postcards throughout the novel, but they reveal so little; like the bear that fronts them, he remains an outsider, disinterested in dialogue, either with his own emotions or the opinions of others (only when near death does he provide a return address). And yet the postcard format speaks volumes, for in his choice of a very public form of communication, rather than the relative secrecy of a letter in which to confess his crime to his parents, he not only creates an alibi, but also ritually brings Billy back to life for others through the process of writing, a fiction sanctioned by the officialdom of the post office stamp.

The same extends to his creation of the fiction that his family are still living together happily on the farm, a delusion that exonerates him for his flight. In Loyal's postcards time stands still, his emotional development cauterized by events on the hill: they let slip his affection for his mother and lack of warmth for his father (when Mernelle picks up one of the first to be mailed she notes without surprise, 'another bear postcard for Jewell, written in Loyal's handwriting' (pp. 40–1)), and a deep-seated hankering for his own family. His Christmas greeting to the daughter of Berg (one of the miners with whom he is trapped in the Mary Mugg), Pearlette, is full of pathos – in his mind she remains a little girl who is the same age as the Mernelle he left behind, a symbol of the family that he can never have and the family he has lost. In writing he realizes that he has nothing to say and the card remains unsent (p. 180).

The tone of the postcards also reveals much about the character of the sender. Mink's tone is bullish and blunt, and whereas his recipients are never addressed by name, his signature reveals his full name, underlined for emphasis. His first card, rejecting the offer of artificial insemination for his stock, screams at the reader with rage and is undercut with irony. On the Blood farm they inseminate the old way, as Loyal has just proven on the hillside. Loyal's actions mean that Mink has lost his favourite son, hence his anger at anything that reminds him of his modernizing efforts. Furthermore, it is unfortunate that the card focuses on bloodlines, for in losing Loyal he has lost his bullish successor. It is bullishness that leads to Mink's downfall: the breathtaking arrogance and naiveté displayed by his hastily filed insurance claim is alarming for the reader, and the outcome is no surprise when the weasel-like Vic Bake takes an interest in the case (pp. 15, 118). Jewell is the opposite: she is unused to writing and when she eventually finds a voice following the death of Mink, it proves uncertain and pathetically ingratiating. Her appeal to Loyal to return, written with the help of Mernelle, is muddled but full of pathos. Her choice of a postcard for such a personal communication indicates that she is uncertain of this means of communication (though here Proulx could be accused of sacrificing psychological realism on the altar of aesthetic consistency), a feeling emphasized by the use of her full name when signing (p. 124). Her card to Dub, by this time a millionaire, thanking him for the gift of a box of grapefruit, is full of pathos. The parenthetical addition of her name after simply signing the card 'Ma', indicates her uncertainty about her role in the family now that all have left her (p. 234).

Dub's cards show him to be ambitious and self-centred. He does not attend Jewell's funeral but posts a cheque for 'the iron railings around the plot' (p. 273). He sends his apologies for not attending the funeral of Mernelle's husband, Ray, with a cliché – 'he was a good man' – before regaling Mernelle with his tax problems (p. 320). Mernelle's postcards chart a history of loneliness and isolation, her passivity and lack of voice symbolized by the fact that we are seldom privy to the contents of her cards, only the replies. From an early age her desperate desire for a pen pal brings her into contact with the predatory Sergeant Frederick Hale Bottum, who reminds us of the dangers for all young girls outside their community, and Juniata Calliota, the daughter of a poor immigrant family. Juniata's family's happiness and ambition (the American dream signified by the 'Old Southern Mansion' that fronts her first postcard) contrasts with her own unhappiness at her dead-end plight (p. 41). Even when Mernelle is married her slightly desperate appeals to Dub to visit suggest her continued loneliness (p. 273).

The postcards of *Postcards* offer a wide variety of interpretations, but although we are encouraged to fill in the gaps, we are also continually being warned of the dangers inherent in such a process. The story of Joe Blueskies is a case in point. When he leaves the narrative, we are unsure whether he is a gnomically taciturn Native American with an ability to conjure a tornado, or a confidence trickster who metaphorically 'scalps' Loyal. Through a series of unconnected postcards spread throughout the novel the reader has the task of piecing together the story of a successful herbalist (p. 135) who was blinded by the storm (p. 333) that blew Loyal's car away (p. 323) and 'removed' the $100 bill from his shoes (p. 253), a narrative that conforms to our romanticized view of Native American characters. However, within the body of the text the reader is offered extra information which leads to another possible interpretation. In the late 1970s, Loyal finds a picture of a man called Walter Hairy Chin in a collection of discarded patient files from a mental asylum in Fargo, North Dakota, and identifies it as the Indian he picked up (p. 276). So who is the man picked up by Loyal: conman, Native American herbalist, or psychiatric patient? We never find out, but our process of piecing together the clues offers a guide to the interpretative strategy of the novel as a whole. In collating the narrative fragments – the pictures, post-cards and anecdotes – we arrive at one of many competing inter-pretations offered by the clues. What follows, therefore, is an unashamedly partial reading of the novel, for Proulx's aesthetic project allows nothing more substantial.

Landscape, and Loyal's tragedy

Postcards, like all Proulx's fiction, begins with a landscape: New England farms dwarfed by mountains that evoke camels and lions resting on the fossil records of dinosaurs. The Blood family is carved out of the inhospitable nature that surrounds them. Our first view of Jewell shows her with 'floral print apron ... beaky nose ... hazel eyes', lips as 'stiff as wood' and 'hands like clusters of carrots' (pp. 6, 8). The landscape smears their jeans, blunts their fingernails, is coughed up in their phlegm, brutalizes and even-tually reclaims them. Mink (whose name reminds us of a quick-tempered member of the weasel family) is crushed by his tractor and has half his ear torn off by a brood sow (p. 11). Dub, too, is disfigured: half his teeth have been knocked out and one of his arms was severed by a train during one of his periodic attempts to escape (p. 10). Throughout the novel, limbs are returned to the land – feet in a mining accident, legs in a riding accident – and then the characters themselves, including Jewell, Mink and Ray, a number of suicides recorded in 'Shotguns' and, of course, Billy.

Loyal, like his dog, is loyal to the land. He grows out of it, is nourished by it, and shapes it:

His blood, urine, faeces and semen, the tears, strands of hair, vomit, flakes of skin, his infant and childhood teeth, the clippings of finger and toenails, all the effluvia of his body were in that soil, part of that place. The work of his hands had changed the shape of the land, the weirs in the steep ditch beside the lane, the ditch itself, the smooth fields were echoes of himself in the landscape, for the labourer's vision and strength persists after the labour is done. The air was charged with his exhalations. The deer he'd shot, the trapped fox, had died because of his intentions and commissions, and their absence in the landscape was his alteration

(pp. 85–6)

The narrator recalls a relationship with the land that is visceral, spiritual and political. Not only is Loyal part of the soil, but he has altered the landscape. John Locke's *Two Treatises of Government* (1689) held that ownership of land came with 'mixing one's labour' with the soil – which became a useful principle for the partitioning of the New World while excluding the Native Americans whose nomadic existence held different concepts of ownership. There is, furthermore, in Loyal's careful husbandry, a spirituality that reaches back to the Christianization of the landscape through the American Transcendentalist movement. As the nascent Republic sought an iconography to make sense of the vastness of the imposing landscape, its writers and painters fell back on old models, transforming the new land into both a Classical Arcadia and, in accordance with the doctrine of Manifest Destiny, the new Eden. In the middle decades of the nineteenth century, this doctrine was given new impetus through the Romanticism of Ralph Waldo Emerson, for whom the sublimity of the American landscape was the very expression of God's grace. Thus, when Loyal takes Billy up the hill to see his pasture – the field he had improved over five years until it stood before him 'propped open towards the south like a Bible' – he is seeking to engage her in a spiritual communion with the land (p. 14).

Or this is what he tells himself later in vindication. For there is in Loyal's reduction of his idealized landscape to a 'gently swelling earth like the curve of hip and breast' a misogyny that reflects a wider strain running through the entire pioneer experience (p. 59); a narrative in which the wilderness is transformed from an Earth Mother into a 'virgin wilderness' which is 'penetrated', 'husbanded' and 'mastered' by men. Billy represents something new, since she is prepared to dismiss Loyal's pasture as being 'like any stupid old field' while refusing, unlike the land, to yield to male domination (p. 14). Indeed, she goes one step further, presenting her virginal body as an alternative site for Loyal's groping exploration in an effort to ease him from the land: 'I'll go just so far with you, and then, if you want what I got, you come the rest of the way with me' (p. 81). It is a fatal game. Loyal's horizons are limited by his need to master the land, and he ends up taking her by force, killing her in the process: the 'Blood temper'. The narrator observes the great irony that she who was 'always yapping about moving away, getting out, making a new start, was staying on the farm. He, who'd never thought beyond the farm, never wanted anything but the farm, was on his way' (p. 13).

The fall

There is in the narrator's presentation of Loyal's crime a symbolic thread that raises it above sordid domestic drama to a level proportionate with Proulx's epic ambitions for the novel.

Immediately following Billy's death the narrator records that 'it was like he'd taken a bad *fall*' (my italics, p. 3); Loyal feels no fear or remorse but experiences an 'abnormal acuity of vision' which leads him to notice the landscape around him – the 'mats of juniper', the 'doghair maple' and the 'humps of moss like shoulders shrugging' – all impassive before his crime (pp. 3, 4). As he 'walked through the withered garden' (the garden motif reminding the reader of the original Fall) it becomes, through a process of pathetic fallacy, reflective of his crime: all is 'rotten bark' and 'deadwood', the roof of the Blood farm is 'a bloom of mould' and 'the mournful smell of rotted fruit came into his nose' (p. 5). Man is a blemish on nature: Loyal 'urinated on the blackened stalks of Jewell's Canterbury bells', and his nostalgic meanderings as he walks through the orchard take him back to a vision of 'his grandfather spraying the tree with Bordeaux mixture, the long wand hissing in the leaves, the poisoned codling moths bursting up like flames' (p. 5). If there is a snake in Eden, it is man with his 'hissing' insecticide dispenser poisoning all around him. Man's culpability is further reinforced by a reference to 'the apple' of original sin with Old Roseboy's advice to a young Loyal: 'Take it easy now, one rotten apple spoils the whole goddamn barrel.' Loyal's blood makes it impossible to 'take it easy', as he is rotten to the core, consumed by the Blood rage that is visited on the sons of the fathers (p. 5).

Billy's murder is not simply contextualized within the myth of the Fall of Man, since it is also placed within the framework of a

Classical tragedy – a feature signalled by such formal features as the five-book structure of the narrative, a section for each decade, which stylistically reflects the five-act structure of the traditional Greek tragedy. Central to this tradition is the heroic struggle of the main protagonist against forces, both internal and external, beyond his control. Viewed through such a lens, Loyal's tragic flaw (or harmatia) is the Blood temper mixed with his own erotic desire, a condition which transforms him from a sordid rapist into a figure deserving of our pity, particularly when his initial crime condemns him to a life of ceaseless wandering, the punishment meted out by offended gods. Thus he becomes a modern Odysseus, the transformation in our perception of him reinforced throughout the text by his continual alignment with a range of suffering characters. Dub's tale of the pilot who survived a night on Camel mountain with just 'a couple [of] cuts' amidst 'guts and arms and legs from nine dead men all around him' is a counterpoint to the suffering of Loyal: he is physically unblemished but in a personal hell (p. 9); he is 'The Bat in the Wet Grass', 'gnashing its needle-like teeth' but unable to escape the coming storm (p. 66); he is 'The Lost Baby' who has not yet learned to crawl backwards and who consequently finds himself trapped in a narrow jam (p. 77); and, ultimately, he is the postcard bear – an outsider with a rough upbringing who becomes a figure of nostalgia while being destroyed.

Proulx's aim in invoking such a tradition is twofold: she is interested in the way that the ordinary man is annihilated by forces beyond his control, whether it is the farmer ruined by modernization, or the moral man destroyed by an act emerging from his ancestral blood. Throughout the novel, Loyal is persecuted by guilt, depicted by the 'black mucky channel that ran from his genitals to his soul [that] had begun to erode', leaving him unable to touch women without a seizure (pp. 58–9). For Loyal, all the troubles that beset him in later life – 'No wife, no family, no children, no human comfort in the quotidian unfolding of his life; for him, restless shifting from one town to another' – are construed as 'the price for getting away' (pp. 58–9). However, Loyal's willingness to interpret his life in such a way points to Proulx's secondary purpose for using the Classical tragedy to frame his experience. Proulx, it seems, is interested in exploring the dark undercurrents of such narratives, whether the misogyny underpinning the 'sacred' relationship between the frontiersman and the wilderness, or, as will be seen in *Brokeback Mountain*, the myth of cowboy 'pardners'. Here, her target appears to be the egotism central to the tragic hero: for to believe oneself selected for special punishment by the gods removes the responsibility for self-analysis. Loyal continually refuses to confront his actions or engage in any form of introspection, a feature symbolized by his inability to write about the death of Billy in the 'Indian's book' (that repository of his intimate thoughts). Instead of dealing with his guilt, Loyal is happier externalizing his feelings through symbols, channelling his remorse into the gesture of freeing a trapped coyote – whose expression, 'mingling appeasement, fear, anger, threat, resignation, pain, horror . . .', captures that of the struggling Billy (p. 296).

In Classical tradition, the voyage of self-discovery was most often presented as a descent into Hades, a journey recreated in *Postcards* through Loyal's experiences in the Mary Mugg. In this subterranean world, where the name of the mine reminds us of female passivity before male exploration, Loyal finds men with a different relationship to the land: men of stone with 'coal for hearts, granite for fists, silver-tongued and [who] liked to see blood' (p. 93). These tastes prove prophetic, as do the words of the Scandinavian fortune teller who had informed Cucumber that he will die by water. As Loyal sits in the darkness waiting like a modern Tantalus for the water to rise, listening to Cucumber bleed out drop by drop '... blood bloodblood blood ...' he believes that his plight is revealed to him (p. 104):

> And now he knows: in her last flaring seconds of consciousness, her back arched in what he'd believed was the frenzy of passion ... Billy had focused every one of her dying atoms into cursing him. She would rot him down, misery by misery, dog him through the worst kind of life. She had already driven him from his home place, had set him among strangers in a strange situation, extinguished his chance for wife and children, caused him poverty, had set the Indian's knife at him, and now rotted his legs away in the darkness. She would twist and wrench him to the limits of anatomy. "Billy, if you could come back it wouldn't happen," he whispered.
> (p. 103)

There is an epic cadence to these lines, brought about largely through the lack of definite articles and third-person pronouns attributable to Billy: this is Loyal's tragedy, his whispered comment eliciting our sympathy. Yet it could be argued that even as he listens to a colleague dying, Loyal remains obsessed with his own suffering, in the process demonizing Billy as an evil witch-like figure. This tendency towards self-absorption rather than self-analysis is signalled by a casually observed piece of graffiti in a late 'What I see' section, 'Write Belerophon', which invokes one of the most heroic of all Homeric wanderers (p. 308). Belerophon's journey began with a murder and led to him facing the hideous fire-breathing Chimera. What an apt symbol of Loyal's own journey, as he transforms his struggle with his own rage into a fight with external agents, agents which are 'chimerical' – or, according to modern usage, fanciful.

What the wanderer sees

In an interview Proulx described Loyal's journey as 'an ironic and miniature version of the American frontier expansion westward', which begins with the formulation of his lie to his parents: 'We're pullin' out and going out west, someplace out there, buy a farm, make a new start' (p. 10). 'We' are not going anywhere, and Loyal is fleeing rather than travelling in hope. And yet the narrator maintains an ironic purity in Loyal's motives, continually invoking a pastoral version of the American Dream in his description of the farm he hankers for: 'The soil would be crumbly and stoneless. There would be a stream with flat rich bottomland on each side for corn and hay crops, and a woodlot ...' (p. 60). It remains an unfulfilled vision every bit as unrealistic as Lennie's dream of rabbits in Steinbeck's *Of Mice and Men*. In truth, Loyal's journey has no destination and the road is less a symbol of hope than a spatial representation of time as he travels from young man to old timer (significantly he dies when his truck eventually breaks down for good). Within the narrative structure of the book, therefore, Loyal's journey becomes emblematic of the movement of the entire nation towards the dystopian vision outlined at the end of the novel; and the 'What I see' sections offer us an opportunity to experience the blurred and dissonant reality of this disintegration.

When Loyal stops his car to take one last glance at his pasture, the reader sees through his eyes nature improved through careful husbandry to form a spiritual relationship between God and men. The landscape through which he journeys initially is still a land of carelessly forgotten hay bales, peregrine falcons, 'miles of vineyards' and swelling cornfields. However, commercialism is already making its mark, with the roadside stores presented to the reader with their capitalized advertisements: 'H&C Café, EATS, Amoco,

GAS 3 MI. AHEAD' (pp. 34–5). These reflections are raised from
the level of simple cultural criticism to some sense of a spiritual
violation by the narrator's observation that tree branches are found
'crucified on wires' and that the voices of a religious programme on
Loyal's radio are breaking up in a world of static. His journey
becomes an epic voyage into spiritual darkness, a sense highlighted
by the night fog and the constantly darkening soil of the fields:
'The earth's colour changes, darker, darker. Prayers and long
silences out of the dusty radio' (p. 35). By the end of the novel, the
beauty in nature is only to be found in the 'laminated scenes of
hunting' which adorn the walls of cheap road-side cafes, while the
land eroticized by Loyal in feminine form is 'erupting with sores'
(pp. 327–8). The whole 'What I see' section in Chapter 54 catalogues these sores, as his journey takes him over a 'crumbling
bridge, exposed cable in frayed rust flowers, past twisted mufflers
and black half-moons of tires'. God is no longer a presence on the
airwaves; radio voices now warn of escaped rapists and polluted
drinking water. It is a land in which dinosaurs have been replaced
by 'behemoth tractor tanks' which spray the land with herbicide
turning it 'deep, deep blue'. The American dream has become a
nightmare, the narrator's mocking 'That's all, folks' highlighting
the grotesque nature of Loyal's dystopian Disney ride (p. 329).

   It could have all been so different, the backroads and mistaken
turnings of Loyal's journey reminding us of periods when men
could have chosen an alternative direction. When, for example, a
confused Loyal takes the wrong road and begins travelling east, he
finds himself going back in time through the pioneer cemeteries of
German and Jewish immigrants – 'Heydt, Hansen, Hitzeman,
Schwebke' – to those so poor that their only decoration is a
corncob (p. 328). At another time he is described on 'gumbo roads
slippery as snot', when confronted with a land of 'fossil tree

trunks' guarded by 'the antelope sentinel's snoring'. It is a land-scape carved as much by the American imagination as by 'ancient water', the sandstone having been 'irradiated' by the hypnotic chants of the Indian war dance, and the air echoing to the hoof beats of 'Red Horse, Red Cloud and Low Dog' as they swept down upon the 'astounded faces of Fetterman, Crook, Custer, Benteen, Reno' (p. 276). In chapter 49 Loyal finds himself on a back road climbing through the fossil records of American development: the jumbled dates from 1838 to 1937 combine with graffiti such as 'Epiphany H. S.', 'Christ will come', '67' and 'Bobby loves Nita' – which takes America from the Founding Fathers to the Cuban Missile Crisis. In the 'howling of the wind' he hears Indian singing, while on the radio he listens to 'I'm Proud to Be an American' (pp. 308–9). The irony seems complete.

Loyal, however, is no mere observer. The need to work means he is continually forging a new relationship with the landscape, which allows the narrator to draw ironic parallels with his crime. Furthermore, the variety of Loyal's jobs also allows the plight of the small independent worker in the post-war era to be examined. Proulx is interested in periods when a community rooted in its landscape starts 'to experience the erosion of traditional ways' as economic conditions change. In *Postcards* this is the post-war per-iod, during which the exodus from the land (accelerated by con-scription) continued unabated, leaving the old, female and infirm grappling with the onslaught of agribusiness. The plight of farming was shared by other rural industries, such as mining (which became the reserve of corporations that could afford the labour and appropriate machinery); local businesses (which suffered from the growth of chain stores); and also rural crafts, such as hunting and trapping (which faced the twin threat of government-funded agents and the anti-fur lobby). To a large extent, Loyal's working history provides a social commentary on a dying way of life. It also becomes part of the epic framework of the novel, as the reader is shown, in true Steinbeck fashion, the tragedy of those battling with economic forces beyond their control.

Loyal's mining career and his time as a uranium prospector, for example, offer the reader a snapshot of industries under threat from big corporations. The Mary Mugg is the remnant of another age, presided over by a grand old matriarch, Mrs Dawlwoody (née Mary Mugg), who leaves it to God to guide her decisions concerning modernization (p. 93). However, the men who mine it like it that way because they consider themselves heirs to a gold-mining tradition of men who could 'read Latin, talk philosophy' and still 'go down in the mines' (p. 96). Their lives are a harmless exercise in nostalgia: they affect the behaviour of nineteenth-century prospectors, Berg riding to work on a mule when he could drive, and Deveaux preferring to make his coffee cowboy-style rather than getting 'a paper cup of coffee from the canteen' (p. 92). It is a far cry from the corporate mines that are always threatening to swallow them up. A similar pioneer dream is apparent in those pimply youths who become uranium prospectors in a modern-day 'gold rush' (Chapter 26). In a landscape 'irradiated' by Indian war chants, Loyal learns to read the land in a new way, locating on maps old Indian 'names like Poison Spring and Badwater Canyon' as indicators of the presence of uranium, and immersing himself in a new mythology of 'lucky strikes' (p. 171). The days of the scratch-dirt prospector, however, are over, the narrator noting: 'It was all big business now, deep mines, acid leaching, chemical extraction, company prospectors, poison wastes and tailings, sand slurry choking the streams, big fish kills and mountains of dead and reeking tailings' (p. 166).

After uranium mining, Loyal turns to bone-digging, working

partly through 'instinct for the way animals might move through a country, part feeling for the millennial landscape' (p.177). Through his views on the footprints he finds, Loyal offers a historical perspective born out of practical knowledge of the land (which is entirely in accordance with *Annales* methodology), which contrasts with the more theoretical approach offered by the university professors. Such men, he argues, 'don't have a feel for the way animals think and move. It's something you got to be brought up with' (p. 183). Loyal understands fear and flight, he remains on the run from imaginary pursuers throughout the novel, and so it is no accident that he should be capable of recognizing the prints made by a dinosaur running in fear. The narrator pushes this symbolism further when an aged Loyal digs up a fulgurite (a rock deformed by lightning), which he takes to be a dinosaur bone. It is entirely appropriate that Loyal should confuse this material symbol of his electrifying rage for part of a skeleton, since it represents the skeleton in his cupboard. It is also characteristic that having uncovered it he should bury it again rather than face up to the consequences of his rage (p. 331).

From bone hunting he turns to trapping. His speciality is the coyote, which throughout the narrative symbolizes the spirit of rebellion – whether through Billy or the feisty Mexican 'Red-Shirted Coyote' on Kortnegger's farm – which generally ends up dead (pp. 258, 296, 315). It is this elusive spirit that Loyal sets out to master, since his own has been corrupted and transformed into rage. His methods, recalled in detail by the narrator and an admiring Dub, are contrasted sharply with the cruelty of the sheep men who blind coyotes before turning them loose to die a slow death, and the government agents who shoot wildly from helicopters or use poison that seeps into the entire food chain. Indeed, in the face of commercial trappers he is less the hunter than the hunted, aligned with the black bear which is driven to extinction for the sake of the aphrodisiacal qualities of its gall bladder. When the Runty Rider (a law enforcement officer determined to root out illegal practices) observes that we will see 'the end of the bears in our lifetime', his judgement resonates beyond the beast itself to embrace men like Loyal, whose craft is also on the verge of extinction (p. 286). Not that the distinction between independent and commercial trappers makes any sense to the urban middle classes; the anti-fur lobby, as Loyal bemoans, proves to be a blunt moral arbiter. Even their most liberal representatives, the hippy characters Paula and Kosti who befriend Loyal the Hat Man, are gently mocked for their inability to listen to Loyal's trapping stories (p. 307).

Eventually, aged 51, Loyal returns to farming, his decision presented in language typical of Biblical and Classical tales of the wanderer's return. Standing in front of the arm of General Alvara Obregón floating in 'a lighted jar of formaldehyde' Loyal understands in a moment of epiphany that losing his farm had been like losing a limb and that 'his way had been that of an exile for a long time' (p. 209). Unable to find land that matches the dream of his pasture to cure his 'trouble with earth', he settles for a 'bony square of dirt' in the North Dakota dustbowl (p. 210). Billy, his loyal dog and his longing for a family are all rolled up into 'Little Girl', a focus for affection which, in another act of symbolic contrition, he risks his life to save (p. 215). However, times have changed, and farming, as his neighbour Old Shears makes clear, has become mechanized. Not only does Loyal lack the machinery, but his farming intuition is inappropriate for the landscape; in planting a windbreak he effectively funnels both the wind and later the burning tumbleweed (caused by the manager of McDonald's trying to clear them from his parking lot with a blowtorch) into his own farm, thus leading to his destruction (p. 221). Once again, it is an episode that appears to be symbolic: the wind-battered tree is a common symbol in Classical, Norse and Native American mythology to represent angry gods. It was also a common image among Romantic writers and painters, particularly those of the American Transcendentalist Movement and the Hudson River School, to show the sublime power of God and the insignificance of man. In the light of such traditions, Loyal's Scotch pines are an act of defiance before the impersonal forces of destiny and it is fitting that he should be punished by balls of fire, which have a particularly Biblical resonance, and exiled once again to the life of the wanderer.

And those that stay at home

Proulx's focus in *Postcards* is twofold: Loyal's observations of an America in which the little man and traditional working practices are under threat, and the experiences of the recipients of his postcards, those left behind. This is the Blood family, left grappling with electrification, increasing mechanization and changing land use; the decline of their farm is emblematic of the disappearance of a certain kind of rural life. This is not to say that the narrator or Proulx sentimentalizes their past. Mink's casual violence; Dub and Mernelle's longing to escape; the catalogue of everyday hardships, help to convince us that Dub is right in believing that 'the farmer's life is a happy life' can only be sung ironically (p. 43). Nevertheless, the narrative is insistent in highlighting the threat posed by outsiders to the delicate rural infrastructure. They create a new relationship with the land, new business practices and a new urban morality that threatens those family and neighbourly loyalties that create the sense of community.

We only see the successful Blood farm glimpsed in the gossip of Mrs Nipple as the 'tight-fenced' operation of the grandfather's day, with 'trotting horses and fine merinos' and three cows for 'family butter and cheese' (p. 23). A combination of war-induced labour-shortage, a fluctuating economy and Mink's stubborn refusal to mechanize has brought the farm to the brink of extinction. And yet the family still maintain a strong sense of community, a product of the brutalizing effects of their environment. Mink, for example, can remember a time when 'relatives and neighbours came without asking to fill in', before adding bitterly just before burning down his barn: 'Where the hell were they now when he was sinking under the black water?' (p. 115). Similarly, when faced with selling the farm, Jewell remembers how the community used to rally round in times of trouble: 'There were so many aunts and uncles, cousins, in-laws, second cousins. All of 'em livin' right around here. They'd be here now, that kind of big fam'ly if it was them times' (p. 126). But when the Blood family are in trouble it is Loyal's childhood friend Ronnie Nipple who comes knocking, exploiting Jewell's sense of family loyalty by pretending that he is purchasing Loyal's pasture on behalf of Mink's brother, Ott. Jewell, who has never grasped the Biblical crime of 'brothers turning their backs on brothers', is totally unprepared for the new world in which neighbourly ties are exploited for commercial gain – and responds to the latter's deviousness in a way that is naive but, to her, entirely appropriate: 'Ronnie. I want you to know you're a decent neighbour' (pp. 128, 127).

Ronnie isn't 'decent' in the sense that she means: he simply understands that in the changing market, family ties possess a new economic value, just as he realizes that the land now possesses value for summer homes, leisure and tourism, rather than dairy farming. Ronnie's profiteering from the land, without ever having touched it, is the very antithesis of the traditional attachment to the land through mixing labour, and signals the arrival of a new and damaging economic morality. As such, the resulting trailer park acts as a microcosm of the mismanagement of the rural environment observed throughout the rest of the novel. The separate lots strike Jewell as looking like a cemetery; by 1969 the site is being polluted with sewage and noise, and when we last see it, through the eyes of Kevin Witkin at the end of the 1980s, it is has become a trailer-trash dystopia, a 'cacophonous symphony of slamming doors. Shouting women, children crying and calling. Saturday afternoon target practice. Assorted trucks, cars, motorcycles, snowmobiles, three-wheelers, ATVs …' (pp. 243, 337).

New people bringing new needs in to a changing landscape – this is what we see through the eyes of Jewell when she eventually takes to the road. And in her critical appraisal it is very easy to hear the voice of Proulx herself:

She saw the landscape changing … She was critical when the road crews cut overhanging limbs from maples. Tears streamed when they cut the trees themselves to widen the highway, hardtop now all the way to the Post Road. The village grew unaccountably, men sawed down the yellowing elms, tore up stumps with great corkscrew machines. The street spread like unpenned water to the edges of the buildings. Metal roofs glittered … The clear-cut left the hills as bare as the side of a scraped hog. The old common became a park with walks and concrete benches already crumbling in their second spring. …

New people owned the general store, started new stores, turned barns into inns and woodwork shops. They moved into farmhouses hoping to fit their lives into the rooms, to fit their shoes to the stair treads. She thought they were like insects casting off tight husks, vulnerable for a little while until the new chitin hardened.

(p. 144)

Seen through Jewell's eyes, all is cutting, sawing, tearing. She focuses on the 'nasal moaning of chainsaws' and hills so radically exploited that they are 'as bare as the side of a scraped hog'. All is now artificial: the Post Road, which evokes a rather more bucolic age, is now tarmac, and it is the house roofs, rather than water, that 'glitter' in the sunshine. The 'old common' has become a 'park' – communal rights having given way to prescribed leisure, the natural world ordered into walkways and concrete benches, the latter 'already crumbling'. Later we learn that the bandstand, a centre for community entertainment, has already disappeared (p. 144). The new people fall into two categories: those who attempt to create a faux-rural lifestyle out of romantic notions of the countryside, and those, like the manufacturer of clumpy pine chairs, Hubbardkindle, who provide the props for this staging and supplement their limited skills with inventive advertising.

In *Postcards*, Proulx is more interested in the former, what she termed in an early essay published in the *Washington Post*, the 'Urban bumpkins': 'Urban Americans [who] idealize the countryside as a beautiful, quiet, healthy, psyche-restorative refuge ... But they do not know how their new rural surroundings work. They do not know where they are, nor do they understand that humans have to fit themselves into a landscape with some care and understanding ... They do not grasp how sharply at variance their perceptions are from those of country people.' *Heart Songs* is full of such characters: men like Earl ('The Unclouded Day'), who has the wardrobe of a game hunter, but the reflexes of a 'snowman'; and the Moon Azures ('Electric Arrows') who create a rural idyll, replacing tin roofs with slate and barbed wire with wooden picket fencing, who cover their walls with carefully framed sepia photographs of the farm's previous owners, and who prove to be so lost in their dreams that they mistake a childish stone carving for an

ancient Native American petrolyph; or the customers of Bill
Stong's outdoor supplies shop, to whom his irascible temper seems
quaintly rural ('On the Antler'). In *Postcards* the urban bumpkins
are the customers of Jo-Jo's Downhill Shop, who buy Jewell's
ghastly knitted stockings, hats and sweaters ('jagged yellow bolts
encircling his torso, red airplanes swooping across a cobalt-blue
breast, endless green reindeer marching over maroon and orange
sleeves' (p. 199)) on the grounds of rural authenticity rather than
taste (p. 196). Most obviously, it is the Boston dermatologist Dr
Franklin Saul Witkin, whose very name implies the bumpkin-like
quality of lack of wit. All are treated by Proulx's various narrators
with indulgent mockery, since their threat is benign and their lack
of understanding of rural ways is continually exposed by wryly
observant locals for humorous effect. This is typified by the
description of Witkin's plans for an idealized log cabin, a place
where he and his brother-in-law, the New York gallery owner Larry
J., can live out boyhood fantasies when 'both dreamed about huts
in the forest' and playing at cowboys (p. 147). As such, they dress
the part and hunt, though the inclusion of Witkin's postcard asking
for insoles for his new cowboy boots suggests that he wants rural
authenticity with comfort (p. 146).

There is something peculiarly American about this connection
between landscape and male relations. It has its roots in the way
the Founding Fathers of the nascent republic, Benjamin Franklin
and Thomas Jefferson, sought to distance the ideal of a pastoral
republic from the decadent urban traditions of Europe. Their
vision was propagated through the work of Emerson who, in
influential essays such as 'Nature' and 'Self Reliance', set out his
vision of the model American citizen as a tough, self-reliant out-
doorsman, capable of penetrating the wilderness and uncovering
its sublime mystery. It was also immortalized in the 'Leather

Stocking' novels of James Fenimore Cooper, in which the wilderness provided a backdrop to a romanticized encounter between man and 'nature', carried out with a male partner, or 'blood brother', usually a Native American, who understands the masculine lore of the Land. Indeed, there is a tradition in American letters, most notably Leslie Fiedler's classic account *Love and Death in the American Novel* (1960), that says that the only important relationships in American fiction are the ones between men pursued in the 'Great Outdoors', exemplified by the friendship of Hawkeye and Chingachgook in *The Last of the Mohicans* (1826), Ahab and Quigueg in *Moby Dick* (1851), and much later by The Lone Ranger and Tonto. Significantly women were no part of this archetype: at best they were symbols of virtue, kidnapped by savage Native American males (women and children are rarely represented), which conveniently silenced them while transforming the partners' search into a quest; at worst, they represented the complications of domesticity and responsibility, everything with which the young pioneer found himself at odds. In later literature this spirit of endeavour and masculine kinship re-emerges in the retreat into nature to hunt and fish with a buddy, which we see in the works of Steinbeck, Arthur Miller and Ernest Hemingway. Such trips are not irresponsible flights for freedom (such as the alternative offered by taking to the road), but a means of reaffirming those positive qualities that forged the nation, away from the influence of women.

This is the tradition with which Proulx appears to be working in her characterization of Witkin and Larry, and later, as will be seen, her characterization of Jack and Ennis. Certainly Witkin's wife has no role to play in their dream, and she in turn dismisses their plans as both impractical and uncomfortable. Even the men themselves are confused by their feelings, and it is the narrator's exploration of this aspect of their character that transforms them from caricatures in to more interesting studies of the way in which male relationships can be altered when displaced from the city to the woods. For although both Larry and Witkin admit to confused feelings among the trees, they believe that at some deeper level their experiences are shared by their partner:

> Only the half brother understood the atavistic yearning that swept [Witkin] when he stood beneath the trees, when a branch in the wind made the sound of an oboe. He had only to walk into the woods far enough to lose the camp, and he was in an ancient time that lured him but which he could not understand in any way. No explanation for his sense of belonging here ... He could hear a little drum, a chant. But what could it mean? The kernel of life, tiny, heavy, deep red in colour, was secreted in these gabbling woods. How could he understand it?
>
> (p. 187)

Both men recognize an irresistible need to go into the woods, yet they are unable to account for it and find themselves puzzled when they get there. For Larry, as his reflections on the conceptual artwork by Joseph Beuys make clear, their discomfort derives from the distinction between the aesthetic contemplation of nature and the practicality of living in it. Witkin, however, is a dermatologist, obsessed with surfaces and appearances. He refuses to engage on an emotional level with his patients because he 'did not like to hear people say how they felt', preferring instead the certainties of removing problem corns and moles with a scalpel to leave the body unblemished (p. 186). But in the woods he finds something different, that all nature comprises of fungal growths, 'bark crevices' and 'split husks' – an imperfect whole that makes no sense to his dermatologist's eye (p. 187). Larry, at least, has the painter's perspective that enables him to distinguish the singularity of different species of bird and tree: to Witkin 'the birds meant as much to him as wild mushrooms, nothing in their singularity' (p. 187). Overwhelmed by this revelation of what he believes is the 'kernel of things' he finds himself withdrawing, first from his patients, then his family and eventually Larry himself (p. 187). It is only the latter's death that relieves him of this numbness by bringing him face to face with his own mortality. Only then does he take a scalpel to the landscape determined to 'put the chaos of nature in order', hiring a stump puller to uproot the trees whose music he once found so beguiling so that he can sow 'grass seed for his lawn in the wilderness' (p. 280). As he draws up plans for a double garage, tool shed and extra bedrooms he returns to the caricatured outsider who is able to romanticize nature only when it is shorn of all its mystery.

And those that got away

At the same time that the narrative describes the destruction of the Blood farm, it also records the desire of two of the Blood children, Dub and Mernelle, to escape. Dub is significant because he lives the American Dream while creating the American nightmare. From the very beginning we know that his desire to get off the land has driven him to 'riding the boxcars', from which he has returned with the most curious souvenirs, the least incongruous being bags of soil for his landlocked family (p. 27). Later in the novel he is revealed to be a lover of things urban – the 'the shriek of jets ... the funky music, the wild toughs, the deals and dirt, the eroding beaches, the sense of being in a foreign and lethal place. Home' (p. 227). He displays little feeling for the land, a characteristic symbolized, as Rood has observed, by his prosthetic arm of 'lifelike' plastic. At the beginning of the story, he is contrasted unfavourably with Loyal and, crushed by his mother's disappointment and his father's contempt, he finds refuge in his role as the family clown. His joking and dancing are a source of some relief in otherwise bleak Blood biographies. Accordingly, we are sympathetic to him as his attempts to find work founder on his disability and as a wedge is gradually driven between him and Myrtle. This sympathy is later re-examined in the light of his subsequent behaviour. For it is this disfigured outcast that the narrator chooses as his new Adam in a re-enactment of the Fall, placing him in a new Spanish 'Garden of Eden' where he is tempted by the sharp-tongued business practice of Maurice Bent.

Maurice Bent represents the type of business motivational speaker who transform greed into a religious vocation. The age and ethnicity of his class seems to have been chosen by the narrator to suggest the melting pot of American immigration. The old business values are represented by John Corcoris, the sponge diver whose business has been undermined by synthetics, and who is looking to real estate to earn enough money 'to raise my family, live comfortable' (p. 164). His conservatism is ridiculed by the predatory Bent, whose name clearly signals his sharp business practice, who is, ironically, a personification of the problems afflicting Corcoris. In tones more familiar on the lips of a prophet, he outlines his dream for the new Eden: 'This class WILL be animated by each student's desire to make a million dollars.' His motto is: 'I refuse to accept the fate life handed me. I will MAKE my OWN fate' (p. 164). This belief in the ability to be reborn – 'Some of you may have had sorry pasts' – stands in sharp contrast to the behaviour of Loyal, who is continually running from his past, believing himself the victim of malign fate. Dub, by contrast, is ripe for conversion: a shiftless character who feels no guilt for his part in his father's death, he is ready to embrace this new vision of Eden (p. 164).

Some seventeen years later, Dub is a similarly tanned, white-suited millionaire enthroned in his 'peacock chair' in his own version of Eden (p. 273). He has made his millions through his cynically named Eden Inc., a real estate company that specializes in transforming untouched landscapes into Disney-style theme parks (p. 226). Aware that he has made a living from sharp business practices that destroy the landscape, replacing rare fauna and flora with 'expensive plastic shit', he remains, however, contemptuously detached (p. 227). Sitting in his plastic Eden he is rich but numb: he has no children of his own, just his properties and his collection of orchids, an ironic choice, as Rood has noted, since it is an exotic flower that grows without contact with the soil. Significantly, in this snapshot the narrator guides us towards his love of the smell of the decaying 'banyan tree' in the centre of his garden, 'with its humped root knees, its branched arms and rooting thumbs, the twists of vine and florid blossom, the mottled, shreddy bark and falling, falling fragments' (p. 275). A description that evokes both a decaying Tree of Knowledge and an image of the crucifixion offers an apt symbol for the rottenness that lies at the heart of this particular version of the American Dream.

This rot emerges in the narrator's detailed description of the Miami riots of 1980 in 'La Violencia', the opening postcard making explicit the link between the cancer that killed Ray and the cancerous city that 'vomited blood' (p. 320). The riot is the ultimate expression of social breakdown, and Dub, who is under investigation from the tax department, is part of the problem, one of the 'money-men and investors fleeing with condos unsold, office towers unleashed, undeveloped properties foreclosed' (p. 321). His wife, Pala, the 'Pirate', becomes the trapped witness to the anger of the mob. Her ordeal is related in a chaos of voices: the cinematic third-person narrative is punctuated with short expressions culled from her later retelling of the event, filleted with the radio announcer's simultaneous commentary. This juxtaposition allows Proulx to criticize the transformation of human suffering into news entertainment through the appropriation of the most gruesome clichés: 'The voice of the announcer went on excitedly as though he were there watching, leaning into the car to notice how much blood there was, or if, perhaps, the tongue was cut out and a red rose jammed into the seeping orifice' (p. 321). As for the community, we have travelled a long way from the time when a whole region came together to search for a lost baby; Pala is a 'lost baby' who becomes the object of grotesque voyeurism. When Dub and Pala eventually leave, the narrator notes that it was the same month that Christo began wrapping the bay islands in a pink plastic: it is a fitting monument to a city consigned to the trashcan, and Dub's egocentricity is signalled by the fact that he can only respond to the artwork by comparing its colour to Pala's bathrobe.

The changing role of women

Throughout the novel, women are presented as a group in a state of transition which reflects the social changes taking place in the 40 years immediately following the Second World War. It is a period of apparent liberation: the war years drew women into the workforce; the decline of traditional heavy industries saw the development of work patterns in which women could compete more equally; the introduction of labour-saving devices freed women from the drudgery of domestic slavery; and the Pill asserted their control over childbirth and sex. However, through her gallery of female characters Proulx explores the limitations of these changes, revealing the ambiguous nature of freedom afforded women in modern America.

The novel opens with the violation and murder of a woman: this act, as we have seen, sets in train Loyal's subsequent adventures within the framework of a Classical tragedy. But in resurrecting this tradition, however, Proulx criticizes the misogynistic reliance upon the violation of a woman to set the hero on his voyage of self-discovery. For Billy is no statuesque Helen of Troy – a passive object of male veneration – but a vivid woman who, in the mould of Curley's wife from Steinbeck's *Of Mice and Men*, has her own agenda for escape. 'I'm not getting caught,' she announces to Loyal on one of their first dates, 'I'm getting out of here and I'm going to be somebody ... I'll go just so far with you, and then, if you want what I got, you come the rest of the way with me' (p. 81). It is a blunt ultimatum, and through it the narrator exhibits the ambition of the newly empowered woman, while also demonstrating its limitations: for she still needs a man to accompany her, and her instrument for securing his compliance is the withholding of sex. Thus, we haven't moved far at all in terms of sexual politics, a feature that the narrator emphasizes by never representing Billy other than through the eyes and memory of Loyal; and his recollection of their first meeting tells us everything we need to know about his attraction and also its fatal limitations:

Even under the trees he saw everything, the pointed fox face, the smart georgette dress with the round white collar, the little jacket with puffed sleeves, a full mouth, lipstick almost black ... She had a strange glamour, like a magazine advertisement, strange and beautiful, standing there dressed all the hell up in front of Ott's tree with its dangling tire swing, the grass spattered with duck shit.

(p. 83)

From the first she is the object of male gaze, less a person than an assemblage of carefully catalogued exotic attributes, contrasted with the mundanity of Middle-American family life – symbolized by the 'tire swing'. He is disconcerted by her, his sexual experience of women being limited to the schoolteacher May Sparks, with her 'flat drooping buttocks and the wide freckled breasts like saucers of cream scattered with droplets of honey', as 'easy to tumble as a rocking chair in the wind' (p. 82). Billy he can only conceive of in terms of advertising clichés, or as a 'fox', a quick-witted animal that must be trapped. Accordingly, his memories of their sexual encounters are confused, fluctuating between symbols of her exotic femininity, such as 'her little shoes with the bows', and his recreation of her as a vivid creature with 'pointed fingernails' and a 'pointed tongue', whose passion is signalled by 'her stinging hail of kisses' (p. 81). Once again, she exists as a collection of physical effects and attributes rather than as a person, making it easy for Loyal to idealize her without ever engaging with her as a person. But this, the narrator implies, is what men do: they are forever squeezing women into a world view that denies their existence as real people. Even her bodily remains are misinterpreted. When her grave is discovered by Witkin, his romantic notions of the Wild West mean that he believes himself to be looking not at the body of a young woman, but at the corpse of a pioneer woman worn out (in his idealizing imagination) by the rigours of childbearing. Nothing could be further from the truth, as the flawless teeth and single, curling shoe would suggest, but it is not for Witkin to let such detailed singularities cloud his impression of the whole (p. 282).

However, 'Down the Road', in Big Pinetree's garage, Loyal is brought face to face with a very different set of sexual relations. With her husband in the Pacific, 'Mrs Big Pinetree' (the label mysogynistically attributed to her by Loyal) runs the garage. Her clothes, 'a man's grey sweater over a housedress printed with seahorses', indicate her transitional status, as does the narrator's extraordinarily detailed description of her making a chicken sandwich, in which the traditionally female activity of food preparation is transformed into bricklaying; even the cut of the bread 'kitty-corner or straight' becomes a site of sexual confusion (p. 30). To Loyal, from whose perspective the scene is narrated, she remains first and foremost a woman to be appraised sexually: 'She was big, but she wasn't bad' (p. 31). Times, however, have changed, and women like Mrs Big Pinetree possess the independence that allows them to be predators, leaving Loyal to reassess his position and draw an equally sexist conclusion: 'She wasn't much, just another penned-up woman who didn't know how to dig her way out, all grease and grits, but ready to give it away to anybody that came by' (pp. 31–2). It is a statement full of irony, not only because it reveals a male-biased disgust at women who actively provoke sexual encounters, but also because the metaphor links her behaviour to that of Billy, a woman who is literally unable to dig herself out. As they return inside to fix the 'bonus', we are presented with a disgraced Loyal grasping onto a rack of bear postcards, gasping for air like he was 'digging a pit on the hottest day' (p. 32). Mrs Big Pinetree may not know how to 'dig herself out', but she succeeds in unearthing the 'curse' of Billy.

The dark side of the matriarchy

The Jewell we meet at the beginning of the novel resembles a rural matriarch in the mould of Ma Joad in Steinbeck's *The Grapes of Wrath*. Power within the family is very clearly delimited, allowing her forthright assertion that 'I don't work to the barn and my girl don't work to the barn. Barn's is men's work. If they can't handle it they can hire' (p. 23). However, whereas Steinbeck presents a rosy picture of mutual respect in which the collapse of the Oklahoma farming community actually strengthens the role of the matriarchy (symbolized in the powerful last scene in which a starving man is suckled by a new mother), Proulx's narrator reveals the dark side by focusing on the limitations implicit in such a role.

Throughout the novel, strong matriarchs are presented as historical fictions rather than present facts. Loyal, the 'Lost Child', is forever idealizing his mother, the narrator presenting us with a snapshot of him in the early 1980s as a sad old man sitting in a booth in Dot's greasy café transfixed by the picture of a 'grand matriarch ... Celistina Falxa' sitting proudly in the centre of her family (p. 294). When Dot asks teasingly whether he has found the 'secret of the ages' she is nearer the mark than she thinks. In Loyal's view, he has: the strong mother holding together her family is everything that he has lost. His hopeless nostalgia is evident in the fact that Jewell, the farm and the family no longer exist – if they ever did anywhere other than in his rosy-eyed view. Indeed, by this date such matriarchs have become the subject not of affection but of academic study, as indicated by Kim Witkin's study of older Sioux women. Her choice of topic is rich with irony, since Kim is the daughter of a man who idealized pioneer mothers, but turned his back on his own wife and family (p. 310).

In truth, the 'matriarchs' that we meet in the novel have a hard time of it, remaining with their husbands not out of loyalty but because social convention prohibits divorce. As Jewell notes: 'It was considered pretty terrible to get divorced, so they put up with a lot, things no woman today would put up with' (p. 202). Jewell does not endure the physical violence that afflicted her forebears (of which, more later), but nevertheless suffers the limitations imposed upon her by an unimaginative patriarch, whose furious anger, she recognizes after his death, 'had crushed her into a corner of life'. Whereas Loyal's Odyssey is all blurred movement, Jewell's life is static, her view from the clothesline reduced to the same 'worn scene, the same fields falling away, the fences, the scalloped mountains to the east, the same thing she has seen since she hung out her first wash here thirty years earlier' (p. 87). Reflecting upon her condition, the narrative voice shifts to embrace the complaints of all women:

Men understood nothing of the profound sameness, week after week, after month of the same narrow rooms, treading the same worn footpaths to the clothesline, the garden ... Men couldn't imagine women's lives, they seemed to believe, as in a religion, that women were numbed by an instinctive craving to fill the wet mouths of babies, predestined to choose always the petty points of life on which to hang their attention until at last all ended and began with the orifices of the body.

(p. 143)

Women's lives are presented in terms of confinement and repetition. Even their attention is 'hung' in a mental act of clearing up. Their role in life is a consequence of their reproductive systems, which allows men to perpetuate the 'religious' belief (an act of faith rather than reason) that women derive an instinctive pleasure from motherhood. It remains, of course, another convenient myth which reaffirms the power of the patriarchy.

Liberation for Jewell comes through the death of Mink and, symbolically, through learning to drive. The orange VW Beetle, with its lime green interior, offers a feminized version of the battered trucks driven by the men in the novel, and 'when she drove', we are told, 'her stifled youth unfurled like a ribbon pulled from a spool' (pp. 142–3). Though her reflections are still articulated using stereotypically feminine imagery, Jewell is keenly aware that driving returns to her the freedom that was crushed in her youth. She now has an autonomy that comes with 'the pleasure of choosing which turns and roads to take, where to stop', as well as 'new eyeglasses' which allow her to forge a different relationship to the surrounding landscape (p. 143). Driving offers a change in perspective: 'All her life she had taken the tufted line of the hills against the sky as fixed, but saw now that the landscape changed ... View was something more than the bulk of hills and opening valleys, more than sheets of riffled light' (p. 143). Crucially, she learns that the view from the clothesline is neither static nor prescribed, but is the subject of individual perception and commensurate to possessing a 'point of view', something that was lost under Mink's patriarchy.

However, the narrator makes clear that Jewell's liberation is not all positive. Mobility, both geographical and social, entails the breakdown of the old community, and with it the dissolution of the respect accorded to matriarchal figures. In the new world Jewell finds herself marginalized and vulnerable, prey to the casual rudeness of the young, a feature illustrated through the preparation of another chicken sandwich. When Jewell stops off at a roadside diner we momentarily find ourselves observing the world through the eyes of an older woman, a world where young waitresses are 'barely civil to older people' and 'slapped down the goods' contemptuously (p. 239). This vulnerability is exposed most cruelly by the young Ronnie Nipple during the sale of the farm, though her subsequent removal to one of his trailers is presented as a more ambiguous fate: while she marvels at the convenience and comfort of her compact living space, she nevertheless becomes a sad, isolated figure with only the 'tinned' voices of the TV set for company – a far cry from the proud matriarch idealized by both Loyal and Kim Witkin (p. 198).

Her death on the logging road in Chapter 38 can be read allegorically: neither she nor society is ready for the amount of freedom that she now enjoys. As the Volkswagen grinds to a halt she finds herself in a hostile nature that 'jabbed', 'choked' and 'clawed' her (p. 242). It is here that she 'wished for Mink. Saw how he used his rage to pull him through difficult work, through a difficult life' (p. 242). This is not a nostalgic appeal to a cruel patriarch, but recognition that his hardness offered some form of protection in such an unforgiving rural landscape. This rather negative conclusion is explored further by the narrator through the fate of the novel's other older matriarch, Starr Sagine. Like Jewell she is on her own, her children, as she tells Loyal, having turned their back on her: 'Them ties was cut too long ago. With blunt scissors' (p. 293). Thus, when her husband dies there is no sense of liberation, instead she immediately finds herself isolated and the victim of threats from local farmers who want her land. Her cynical observation that 'a woman wants to learn what kind of neighbours she's got, let her husband die' simply underlines the fact that the breakdown of the old community spirit has left in its wake a selfish culture where the old, the weak and women are exploited (p. 292). Her act of presenting her husband's old 'pearl gray cowboy hat' to Loyal suggests that in such a rural environment a benevolent patriarchy is preferable to the creeping new business-oriented and individualistic America (p. 293).

In the novel the narrator charts the death of the traditional matriarchy, not least by the Blood-line ending with Mernelle. Billy rejects the vision of a future aged 'forty with a big belly every year and kids all over the place', and Pala turns her properties into her family (of which, more later). Mernelle, however, wants something different: she offers a compromise between the exotic dreams of Billy and the next generation of rural mothers symbolized by the schoolteacher May Sparks (p. 81).

Love and death in America

The Mernelle we are introduced to at the beginning of the novel is a quiet, thoughtful girl. She is withdrawn from school to help on the farm after Loyal's departure and is forced to live according to 'Mink's monotonous ideas and narrow corridors of toil'. She is also, we find out late in the story, prey to the predatory attentions of older men, the sexually notorious Toot Nipple 'rubbing his hand over her heinie when she was on the ladder in the barn' – the kind of casual abuse that abounds in Proulx's isolated rural communities (p. 203). Such experiences mean that she develops wisdom beyond her years, fobbing off the request from her potential pen pal, Sergeant Hale Bottum, for a swimsuit photograph by sending a picture of her cousin, Thelma (p. 41). She also develops a reluctance to ignore the macabre side of life, a trait clearly evident during the reader's first encounter with Mernelle as a central protagonist in Chapter 6. Here, the reader follows Mernelle's thoughts as they drift from the reason that Mink parks the truck at the bottom of the hill in November to the voice of Jewell heard behind his actions, a voice that she immediately associates with dark stories: '"Leave the truck up here, we run the risk of bein' trapped for the winter." ... That was Jewell talking through Mink's mouth. Jewell was the one afraid of accidents and fire, had seen her father's barns burn down with the horses and cows inside. Had seen her oldest brother die after they pulled him out of the well, the rotten cover hidden by years of overgrown grass. She told the story in a certain way' (p. 39). Her ability to replay the latter story, as on an old recording, indicates that she is both steeped in a family narrative of suffering and fascinated by it. She is constitutionally unable to see the beauty of the snow around her without reflecting on its potential for tragedy. Indeed, it is like the lush grass covering up the fatal well that kills her uncle.

In a novel so concerned with the darkness beneath the veneer, Mernelle learns early on to ignore the latter. In the chapter 'Tickweed' Mrs Nipple falls to her death through rotten floorboards, Jewell commenting archly, 'when I think how all that rot was layin' there under that proud housekeepin' . . . There's a lesson in it' (p. 77). There is, and it comes to Mernelle as she mourns Mrs Nipple's death while wandering alone in a blooming field of tickweed. Even in this natural Eden, Mernelle proves to be too much a child of the soil to be able to believe that 'Mrs Nipple is an angel . . . and thought instead of the body dissolving into the earth, thought of the earth crawling with invisible hungry mites that devoured rotting bits' (p. 79). Not for her the comfort of adult lies, but she has instead a recognition of death and pain as part of the natural process: 'Where does it go, she thought, all those rivers of menstrual blood and the blood of wounds and injuries from the beginning of the world, imagining a deep, stiff lake of coagulated blood' (pp. 79–80). Life, she concludes, is like the tickweed: a beautiful bloom masking a weed, a conclusion that so horrifies her that 'she ran at the coreopsis, tearing at their heads' (p. 80).

This momentary revelation colours her desire to escape from the farm, as she notes in a Billy-like fashion: 'What am I supposed to do, rot here in this place?' (p. 133). Escape comes initially through the postcards that she exchanges with her pen-friend 'Juniata Calliota' and then through marriage to Ray MacWay. Like so many events in the novel, the narrator guides us towards a mixed response to Mernelle's actions. Despite our dismay at the abandonment of community ties, the vulgar commercialism of 'love' epitomized by this particular 'personal interest story', and our suspicions of Arlene Greenslit's motives, we are forced to concede that Mernelle is demonstrating the kind of willingness to mould her own future advocated by Maurice Bent. Furthermore, her choice of Ray is based less on schoolgirl dreams of romance than on a pragmatic assessment of what he won't do: 'I know he'll never hurt me. I've never seen *him* loose his temper' (p. 139). However, even on their first date we are warned through the image of the trapped bumblebee that the marriage may not be all Mernelle hopes it to be. As it buzzes in front of the glass panel of the kitchen door, it is prevented from entering the 'nirvana' of the garden by the seemingly invisible 'malignant force' (p. 137). A snapshot of their later life together identifies the malignant force that prevents Mernelle from entering her marital nirvana as sterility, both physical and psychological. The narrowness of Mink's patriarchal authority is replaced by the stifling comfort of a suburban dystopia in which her 'blighted longing for kids' is replaced by 'the flickering story' watched on television from 'leatherette recliners' (pp. 244–5). Her life is spent waiting for Ray to come home from work; significantly, despite Jewell's advice, she never learns to drive. Her former attachments intrude only in a sterile parody of themselves: autumn scenes exist in brass frames; Juniata is echoed in the canned Latin American trumpet music; Loyal in Mernelle's hideous bear collection; and her former schoolgirl ambitions in Ivy Sunbeam, the heroine of a child's bedtime story that she would never get to tell.

In fact, another story is more pertinent to Mernelle's life, that of Toot Nipple. We never meet him; instead the narrator allows his story to be revealed through the careful orchestration of internally related anecdotes. He is mentioned peripherally as early as Chapter 2, but despite Mernelle's constant badgering (which has the effect of raising our own curiosity) his story is not told until it is related by Jewell in the eponymous Chapter 31; and even then we are forced to question its veracity since it was undoubtedly picked up from Mrs Nipple. It is a story about sex, death and fate, to which blood remains common. As the two clean fruit, their fingers dripping with the juice of the 'naked bleeding strawberries', Jewell relates the story of the young, handsome womanizer whose love of sex leads him to go out on the 'toot' even when married (p. 204). In his mid-40s, however, he contracts prostate cancer and is forced to choose between death and impotence. He chooses the latter, but becomes withdrawn, refusing female comfort because he is unable to conceive of relations with women without sex. Ironically, he finds himself turning to his wife, but this is only because he cannot face the thought of suicide alone and is seeking company, a request that she deftly avoids. Divine justice, some might say – but Jewell goes beyond this moralistic reading, instead interpreting Toot's demise as a vindication of her own fatalistic belief that 'life twists around like a dog with a sore on his rear end that he bites at to make it stop plaguin' him ... You're never ready for it when it turns on you and goes for the throat' (pp. 203–4). Mernelle, like Loyal, is bathed in the Blood fatalism, a feature demonstrated symbolically through her desire to 'squeeze until the juice ran down her arms'. It is also an action that she recognizes comes from an 'unaccountable and strange wish, like her longing for children' – the peculiarity of the pairing suggesting that fate has brought her miscarriages, which she has learned to face with grim humour: 'they had the dog, she thought derisively' (p. 203).

Significantly, we next see Jewell just before her death in the mountains, the narrator reminding us of the Blood fatalism by having her 'clench[ing] wild raspberry canes' for support in her last moments (p. 242). The next snapshot of Mernelle, after her stifling meal with Ray, is at his deathbed: life has come back to bite them both. The narrator makes clear life's cruel injustice by drawing out parallels with Toot Nipple: the callous, oversexed Toot, unable to conceive of human contact as anything but sexual, is compared unfavourably with the kind, but, we speculate, sterile Ray, whose cancer is likened to 'a cow's afterbirth' sucking the life out of him (p. 310). Furthermore, despite his unworthiness, Toot's wife is able to grieve his death, whereas Ray's drawn-out suffering forces Mernelle to actively encourage him to die. Death returns both from sanitized suburbia to their rural roots, for although Mernelle accepts the approach offered by the 'Coping with Death' seminar in which 'Moira Magoon made death sound sensible, a logical decision one could make', and although she tries the 'soft cancer voice' to lull Ray into sleep, it is only when she returns to her 'own scratchy iron' with the abrasive 'you quit fighting, now' that both are able to face death (p. 311).

The successful career woman?

Pala offers a very different example of female evolution, and it is therefore appropriate that she is introduced to the reader through a job interview in which her ambitions, talents and motivation are dissected by a man – this time Dub. Like Loyal when faced with Billy, we again see a Blood disconcerted by an emancipated female: we view her through Dub's eyes, a series of attributes – 'her ivory face, her black oval eyes ... there was a cool glaze he loved' –

assessed by the degree to which he finds them appealing (p. 205). While he focuses on the way her 'hair is plaited', she, like a female version of Vic Bake, talks business with such surety that 'he felt himself the fool again' (p. 205). His recurrent thought, 'she was so serious', provides a typically gendered response which conveniently transforms the female professional into a hard, humourless character. He hires Pala because he is attracted to her, the prefacing postcard warns us of this, but it is also clear that he recognizes that she will be good for business. Marginalized by both her gender and ethnicity, Dub's moniker for her, 'The Pirate', indicates those qualities of cunning and corrupt practices required to make it in a man's world.

Pala is a success in business, but by the end of the novel she is presented to us as a restless unfulfilled figure. While Dub retires to his orchids, 'she had to work. Couldn't retire. Didn't want to retire' (p. 321). She has been forced to sacrifice a great deal to achieve this success: whereas Mernelle hankers for a child, Pala actively chooses not to have children, Dub speculating that 'there might have been an abortion' and then concluding ambivalently that 'the properties were her children now' (p. 274). Furthermore, the narrator is critical of the cold, uncompassionate character that she becomes. When she becomes the victim of the attempted carjacking in the Miami riots, the car becomes less a symbol of female liberation than of social detachment. Significantly, we are not guided towards any sympathy for Pala's vulnerability – indeed, she is not Pala, but 'The Pirate' – but rather condemnation for her disdain for the rioters, one of whom she cripples unnecessarily (p. 321). The city has fallen into anarchy, but Pala is happier to think of it in terms of a Latin-American pseudo-Biblical apocalypse – 'LA TRISTEZA DE MIAMI' – which excuses the part played by her kind of business practices (p. 320). Worse, she views the trouble as a business opportunity, since she now dreams of running a travel agency (a business helps people to run away).

Through the lives and experiences of the female characters in the novel, the narrator is not advocating a return to the myth of the cosy matriarchy exploded at the beginning, but warning that as the role of women evolves socially and economically from its rural roots there is a danger of replacing family and community ties with sterile suburbia, and confusing greater emancipation with naked self-interest.

The trouble with men

If women are presented throughout the novel as a group in transition, then the men remain depressingly set in their ways. Proulx is happiest when writing from a male perspective, but many of her male characters have little to recommend them. The older generation of patriarchs presented to us through occasional anecdotes are drunken, callous and cruel, dominating their wives through irrational displays of violent temper. On his deathbed, Ray recollects among other fugacious images 'the fury of the drunk father', while Arlene Greenslit's father was such a heavy drinker that his mother commemorated his death with a tombstone shaped like a whiskey bottle (pp. 136, 312). Late in the novel, Loyal takes a job under the psychotic Kortnegger, the narrator introducing him while in the midst of a dispute with his wife over cleaning. As the narrative perspective switches momentarily to offer his thoughts, his explosive nature is captured in the succinct observation: 'She was asking for it. His hands throbbed' (p. 314). As always with Proulx, it is the short anecdote that is most revealing, Jewell's tale of an incident between Mink's father, Old Matthew, and his wife clearly demonstrating his appalling character. When Old Matthew finds himself unable to attract the attention of his partially deaf wife, Jewell recalls how he flared up 'like a turkey cock with his face gobbled up so red' and smashed a glass jar of tomatoes on the clean kitchen floor in order to get her attention (p. 202). It is a small example of petty intolerance, but it clearly removes the gloss of the 'good old days'. Such men abound in Proulx's fiction, two notable examples being, as will be seen later, the fathers of Ennis and Jack in *Brokeback Mountain* – 'stud ducks' who govern their families through fear.

In *Postcards* it is Mink who inherits the role of intransigent patriarch, Dub continually lampooning his 'I-was-born-on-this-farm,-I'll-die-on-this-farm,-farmin's-the-only-thing-I-know' attitude (p. 48). He has also inherited the Blood temper, a feature illustrated by incidents such as his casual killing of the family cat, Spotty, which had 'made the mistake of rubbing against [his] leg when his temper was up', and 'the knock down slaps, the whalings he gave the boys, same as he'd had himself' (p. 18). Such violence is endemic, part of the fabric of growing up in this rural community; as a bemused Mink tells Jewell while justifying breaking the nose of the three-year-old Loyal for spilling milk: 'We got to start him young. We got to. It's for his own good. I went through it. And guarantee you he won't spill no more milk.' Jewell's chilling reflection at a later date, 'Nor had he', indicates a recognition that at some level the harshness of rural lives requires a particularly tough education (p. 18). Unfortunately for Mink, violence is all-consuming, the departure of Loyal finds rage 'spurting out of him like jets of water from a kinked hose', before he mindlessly turns his rifle on Loyal's Holsteins in an act of symbolic revenge (p. 17). Jewell, reflecting upon this act, notes that 'Mink's anger seemed to her so wasteful he would have to burn for it in hell', which is, in the burning barn, the fate that befalls him (p. 17).

Mink is generally an unsympathetic character, and yet in the build-up to his decision to burn down the barn the narrator goes some way to rehabilitating him in the reader's eyes by giving us access to his thoughts. Seated in the barn in the midst of milking, the narrator focuses on Mink's half-remembered image of himself as a child standing with his father and his friends as they talked gravely, rifles in hands, while looking anxiously at a pig on a straw bed. The significance of this meeting initially eludes him, but eventually he remembers that the pig had been suffering from Mad Itch and had torn a hole in its side, and that his father was debating whether to put it out of its misery. Momentarily the parallels between his present predicament and the memory of the pig bear down on Mink. All his life he has been surrounded by suffering: his mother, like the pig 'arched in a hoop of pain', trapped in her arthritic body and needing to be put out of her misery; Dub, 'crippled, divorced, a father who'd never seen his son ... always a fool. A goddamn periodical with the boozing'; his own feeling of entrapment, 'poorer every year, the work harder, the prices higher, the chances of pulling out of it fewer and fewer'; and, to cap it all, the very cows he is milking are literally suffering from the Mad Itch (pp. 116, 115). While not exonerating Mink's behaviour, these incidents go some way to explaining his rage: he has been brutalized by a hard life, a fact that Jewell acknowledges in her dying moments. His end is inglorious: torn from the land, betrayed by both of his sons, sharing a prison cell with a predatory homosexual, he turns his rage upon the only person available – himself.

Loyal, of course, inherits the Blood temper, which is perilously interwoven with his sex drive, making it impossible for him to touch women unless, as in the case of Marta in Criddle's bar, he is fighting them (p. 236). As he tries to bring into perspective the relationship between violence and love following the fight he is left to speculate 'how many ways there were to love' – a depressingly sinister train of thought (p. 236). Despite glimmers of hope, such as in his late relationship with the widow Starr Sagine, he remains an outsider. He turns away from the role of husband, with its shared intimacy, symbolically refusing Jack's cowboy hat in favour of the role of itinerant hat man, and a life of corner tables in greasy cowboy diners. In truth he realizes that he can never change, his inability to form meaningful relationships with women is in the blood. Even when close to death, love and brutality are eerily intermingled for Loyal. One of our last views of him is a picture of innocent pleasure as he dances happily in a meadow with the branch of a tree shaped like an imaginary woman, which is interrupted when he falls: '"trip me, you bitch. Get out." Panting, retching with the cough. And hurled the branch, glad to see it break in a spray of red pulp. His loneliness was not innocent' (p. 331). Not innocent, and, rather more depressingly, not isolated – a feature that the narrator makes clear by linking his behaviour to that of the reported rapist.

The book ends as it begins, with the violation of a woman on Loyal's pasture: the consequence of Loyal's crime is visited on subsequent generations. This time we are given the woman's perspective, the anonymous red-haired victim recounting to her ex-husband on the terrace of the Silver Salmon restaurant how the perpetrator had promised a country weekend when 'we'll live off the land and it'll be lovely' (p. 334). Loyal is symbolically present in the form of the shambling bear searching through the food bins outside. The identity of the rapist remains a mystery, yet, as with the narrative as a whole, the reader is able to assemble pieces of evidence to suggest a suspect. For me, Witkin's son, Kevin, offers the most likely candidate. Not only does this reading explain

Kevin's psychological meltdown in Chapter 57, but it also strengthens the novel's narrative symmetry. Through Kevin we see Witkin's atavistic yearning distorted into Loyal's sexual rage, a feature symbolized by the impression of the woman's profile left in the moss 'filling up with muddy water' – a particularly gruesome image of male sexual aggression (p. 335). Kevin's rage is irredeemable; whereas Loyal is allowed to return to his unblemished pasture in his dying vision in the very last paragraph of the novel, in our final view of Kevin, he is in the midst of the Woodcroft Trailer Park taking pot shots at passing aircraft in a display of impotent rage every bit as useless as Mink's shooting of the Holsteins (p. 339).

Loyal's sexual aggression is shared by Kevin, but his emotional isolation is shared by many men in the novel. Throughout we are presented with a gallery of 'Lonely Heart Prisoner[s]', some of whom would not look out of place in Sherwood Anderson's *Winesburg Ohio*. The men described to us by Old Shears in the chapter 'Shotguns' are colourful caricatures who prove Proulx's point that a combination of harsh landscapes, isolation and loneliness reduce human beings to their base elements. C. C. Pope is typical: 'Seventy-four years old, didn't know any women except the two old Prune sisters', falls in love with his Swedish Masseuse, 'big fat woman, a grandmother six times, and about as romantic as a cow flop', but finds himself unable to send the multitude of love letters that he writes, shooting himself instead (p. 231). His lack of emotional articulacy is shared by the taxidermist Charles V. Sunday (his vocation reflecting his inability to deal with living things), and those who provide the 'Human Interest' stories for Arlene Greenslit's column in the *Trumpet*, such as the 'guy who fell in love with a friend of his mother's' and 'shoots her dead' when he fears it is not reciprocated (p. 137). Ray MacWay, of course, finds a less dramatic way to articulate his emotions – advertising for a wife, while characters such as Deveaux, one of Loyal's colleagues in the Mary Mugg, seem to be searching for a mother figure.

Whatever the cause, it is clear that the men in *Postcards*, and indeed in Proulx's fiction in general, have difficulty coming to terms with their emotions, particularly confiding with women. Happy couples are rare in the novel, and men are seldom depicted in domestic situations, usually found instead in the wilderness, in the company of other men. Bullet Wulff has two daughters and a dry-cleaning business, but reinvents himself as a plains drifter and bone hunter with his buddy Loyal; Berg, another of the miners in the Mary Mugg, lives out his fantasy of being a latter-day gold-digger by riding to work on a mule that shares his daughter's name, giving us an uneasy sense of his confused priorities; and, as we have seen, Camp Woodcroft becomes an 'ear trumpet' through which the emotionally inarticulate Witkin and Larry can 'understand each other' away from the pressures of family life (p. 147). Ben Rainwater's observatory is a variation on the hunting camp, a refuge from the feminine where men can drink and indulge in childhood fantasies. Astronomy, however, also provides an apt literary metaphor for a particularly gendered response to the nature of personal inquiry, whether it is into 'The Troubles of Celestial Bodies' or the problem of interrogating personal feelings. Loyal and Ben are transformed into monocular beings, staring perplexedly through high-powered telescopes (instruments that have their own Freudian implications), as they categorize, quantify and map in an attempt, rather like Witkin in the woods, to get to the 'kernel of things'. It is here, dwarfed by the stellar universe, and before the drunken gaze of Ben, that Loyal comes closest to admitting to his crime – but he steps back from self-revelation when the talk turns to psychiatry. This is the problem with Proulx's men: their emotions are either buried (in which case they find expression in alternative ways) or projected onto an epic scale (which allows them to distance themselves from the consequences of their actions). They are never the subject of domestic discussion, an option which would trivialize the singularity and scale of their personal suffering (pp. 194–5). It is this emotional suppression that Proulx will repeatedly return to in her fiction, most notably in her short story *Brokeback Mountain*.

3

The Story: *Brokeback Mountain*

Brokeback Mountain originally appeared in *The New Yorker* magazine in October 1997. It had initially been sent to a competitor, but they dithered over publication for months: *The New Yorker*, on the other hand, accepted in hours. The story emerged, Proulx recalls in her essay 'Getting Movied', (*Brokeback Mountain: Story to Screenplay*) during an evening in a bar in early 1997 when she spotted an older ranch hand sitting on his own, who seemed preoccupied with the young cowboys playing pool: 'There was something in his expression, a kind of bitter longing', which provided the germ for Ennis del Mar. Her thoughts were shaped further a few weeks later when she overheard a bar owner ranting about the recent visit of two 'homos', which concluded with the menacing observation that it was lucky that most of his regulars had been away at a darts tournament, otherwise 'things would have gone badly'. She began to consider what it would have been like for 'any ill-informed, confused, not-sure-of-what-he-was-feeling youth growing up in rural Wyoming'. The state, she claims, is notoriously homophobic, like 'any rough, outdoor-oriented society, where work and physical competence and the masculine rules are the order of the day... it's in the air, it's in the water'. She cites as evidence the homophobic murder of the student Matthew Shepard just outside Laramie in the year after the story was published, and the alarmingly high suicide rate in Wyoming among single, elderly men.

She decided to set the story in the early 1960s, presumably because such rural homophobia stood in stark contrast to the universal liberation sweeping the country's cities, and also because Ennis and Jack would have grown up in the repressive 1950s. It was important for Proulx that they were clearly homophobic themselves, especially Ennis, and that they wanted to be cowboys – part of the great Western myth. She is adamant, however, that this is not a story about 'gay cowboys', but 'a story of destructive rural homophobia'. She recollects how she did most of the 'writing' when driving, a middle-aged woman struggling to empathize with, and catch the speech rhythms of, two rough, badly educated farmhands. 'It was a hard story to write,' she recalls, the manuscript going 'through more than sixty revisions' as she sought 'the right phrase or descriptor for particular characters'.

Such painstaking care and attention make her addition of an entirely new opening for the book publication worthy of particular attention. Set in Ennis's trailer and deliberately divided from the main text through its italicized format, it has the immediate effect of transforming the subsequent story into a flashback. In effect, she conjures up the sad figure in the barroom, presenting us with the shattered results of the rural homophobia that she is about to record. Inside the trailer, all is shuffling shoddiness, Ennis drinking left over coffee, urinating in the sink, dressing without washing – while outside the hissing, roaring, booming wind prepares us for an epic encounter between Ennis and forces beyond his control. The passage is designed to pique the reader's curiosity, Proulx's narrator refers to characters and objects – Jack Twist, a married daughter and also 'the shirts' and 'the mountain' (the definite article emphasizing their importance) – in a manner that implies the reader's understanding but in fact abruptly forces the reader into an entirely new world. This world is dominated by the twin possibilities: seedy bachelordom, with its 'stained cups' and 'chipped enamel pans', and the dreams that might warm the heart if given time (p. 283). The critic Henry Alley has argued in his essay 'Arcadia and the Passionate Shepherds of *Brokeback Mountain*' (Published in Jim Stacy's illuminating collection *Reading Brokeback Mountain: Essays on the Story and the Film*) that the scene offers Ennis some sense of closure by 'suggesting that he has found some solace in his dreams of Jack and in his relationship to his married daughter' (p. 15). But there is no closure here, simply the sad spectacle of the shattered remnants of a human being, buffeted by both the elements and economic conditions that force him to stay with his daughter, who is wedded to a dream that, while pleasurable, exposes those elements of his own character that he most condemns.

The importance of Brokeback Mountain

Like *Postcards*, landscape is central to the story of *Brokeback Mountain*, a fact indicated most obviously by the title, as well as observations made by the characters within the text, most notably Jack's comment that 'old Brokeback got us good' (p. 299). Proulx herself has noted:

In my mind isolation and altitude – the fictional Brokeback Mountain, a place both empowering and inimical – began to shape the story. The

mountain had to force everything that happened to these two young men
... In such isolated high country, away from the opprobrious comment and
watchful eyes, I thought it would be plausible for the characters to get into
a sexual situation.

Proulx's evocation of a specific landscape conducive to the
flowering of male love has a long literary and artistic history, and the
critics Henry Alley, Ginger Jones (Stacy) and Eric Patterson (*On
Brokeback Mountain: Meditations about Masculinity, Fear, and Love in the
Story and the Film*) have all made clear her debt to such a tradition.
The Greek poet Theocritus (310–260 BC) described in his *Idylls* a
mountaintop land of 'idyllic' beauty in which male love, through a
form of pathetic fallacy, is both naturalized and sanctioned. It re-
emerges as the Arcadia of Virgil's *Eclogues* – a land of pastoral beauty
(pastoral deriving from the Latin for shepherd) in which evenings
are spent drinking, playing the pan pipes and telling tales of heroes;
it is a masculine world in which women are only present in the form
of woodland nymphs. It is a landscape that has become in the
European artistic imagination the ideal location for the exploration
of male relationships. The *Eclogues* of both Dante and Petrarch
explore the notion of strong Platonic love in a pastoral landscape;
while John Milton mourned the death of a student friend with his
elegy *Lycidas* (1638), which saw them both transformed into
shepherds. In the repressive nineteenth century the pastoral elegy
became the accepted means of exploring male relationships: Shel-
ley transformed the dead Keats into *Adonais* (1821), and Matthew
Arnold turned Arthur Hugh Clough into *Thyrsis* (1866). In his
Calamus poems, as Patterson has noted, Walt Whitman removed this
tradition to America, seemingly recognizing in the splendour and
marginality of the untamed American landscape a freedom for male
love to express itself away from social condemnation.

It is clear that through her descriptions of Brokeback, with its 'great flowery meadows' and 'glassy orange' dawns, Proulx is seeking to invoke this tradition (p. 287). The fact that Jack and Ennis tend sheep rather than herd cattle softens the rugged cowboy aesthetic, reminding us of those countless Claude Lorrain landscapes of contented shepherds, nurturing and protecting their flocks. Brokeback offers a mythical realm where they 'believed themselves invisible' looking 'down on the hawk's back and the crawling lights of vehicles on the plain below, suspended above ordinary affairs ...' (p. 291). It is this sense of isolation that, as Proulx has suggested, enables them to challenge the gods, or, more prosaically, to defy both social convention and internal quibbles in the development of their relationship. Encoded in the Arcadian allusion, however, is the tradition that defiance entails retribution: the mountain air is both 'euphoric' and 'bitter' (p. 291). The narrator further emphasizes the dangers of defiance through Jack's admission that the feather in his hat came from an eagle shot the summer before (p. 286), a symbol that aligns him with mythical wanderers such as Coleridge's Ancient Mariner (whose shooting of an albatross condemns him to years of storms), and, as Jones has noted, with the myth of Hercules, whose act of shooting an eagle is punished when his male lover Hylas disappears, leaving Hercules with only a shirt for remembrance.

The relationship between pastoral pleasure and the threat of retribution is also played out in the Christian story of the expulsion from the Garden of Eden, a myth that we have already seen in *Postcards* and one which is invoked here in the narrator's description of Jack and Ennis's descent from the mountain. There is an Old Testament resonance to the narrator's description of the way that the mountain 'boiled with demonic energy' projecting Ennis into what he describes as a 'headlong, irreversible fall' (p. 292).

The connection between the American landscape and the Fall has always weighed heavily upon the imagination: though the first Puritan settlers could convince themselves that they had arrived in a new Eden, they could not blind themselves to the evil that lurked in the dark woods, made manifest by the presence of Indians and the activities of witches (a tension explored in Nathaniel Hawthorne's *The Scarlet Letter*). One particular source of evil to Christians is same-sex love, which, while presented as natural and innocent in pagan pastoral literature, is, ironically, condemned in the Christian tradition as a crime against nature. Thus, by invoking the Fall, the narrator not only prepares us for the condemnation that Christian society will level at Jack and Ennis, but he also turns the myth, which is a celebration of heterosexual relations, on its head. In their pre-lapsarian garden Jack and Ennis eat Forbidden Fruit and gain knowledge about themselves, which they do not repress but transform into love. The snake in the grass is not 'Jack Nasty', as Alma later terms him, but Aguirre, whose surveillance provides a constant reminder of social taboos, and who is directly responsible for bringing them off the mountain early (p. 303).

There is, however, a third aesthetic that Proulx appears to be invoking in her foregrounding of Brokeback, a form of American Pastoral that has its roots in the myth of the frontiersman. We have already noted, during our examination of Witkin and Larry in *Postcards*, Proulx's interest in the way in which the retreat into nature offers urban males an opportunity to form close bonds while reaffirming those pioneer qualities of hardy self-reliance that are central to the American male identity. In *Brokeback Mountain* this is taken one stage further, as Proulx invokes the ultimate symbol of this tough, masculine spirit, the Texas cowboy. From her earliest conception of the story, Proulx is clear that it is important that both Jack and Ennis 'wanted to be cowboys – part of the great Western myth', because it enabled her to make explicit relationships which she considered implicit in the genre.

For Proulx, as she made clear in her article 'How the West was Spun', the cowboy is a triumph of propaganda. Following the Civil War, the flourishing 'dime novel' market sought a new hero and took the foul-mouthed illiterate cowhand, many of whom were African American and Mexican, and transformed him into a symbol of 'individual freedom, independence, toughness and pioneer "spirit"'. Through the canvases of George Catlin and Frederick Remington, the Wild West spectacles of Buffalo Bill Cody, and hugely popular novels, such as Owen Wistler's novel *The Virginian* (1901), the cowboy emerged as the archetype of masculinity: a man of action and few words, a free agent (sometimes an outlaw in the case of Jesse James and Billy the Kid), who would employ his gun-slinging skills for the good of the community (to which he remained at best ambivalent), before riding off into the sunset. It is an archetype reinforced through Hollywood cowboys portrayed by John Wayne and Clint Eastwood. Women played little part in such mythology; instead they were equated with domesticity, family responsibilities, the need to earn a living and, by extension, the urban. The only acceptable woman, apart from the symbol of virtue kidnapped by 'Red Indians' to galvanize the cowboy into action, was the frontier prostitute (the hard woman with a heart of gold and wisdom beyond her years who would often end up marrying the cowboy; an equally mythical creation), whose transient ways fit in with the cowboys' itinerant lifestyle. The only real emotional attachment for the cowboy was to his horse and his 'pardner' – the latter, particularly when a Native American, often becoming a 'blood brother' through an act of ritualistic male bonding. The death of either horse or 'pardner' precipitated a display of manly emotions combined with a justification for the cowboy's vengeance.

Proulx's story, then, is less a 'cowboy story' than an exploration of the relationships implicit in the representation of 'storybook cowboys'. Jack and Ennis aren't really cowboys at all, they are about a hundred years too late, and they do not even herd cattle; they have simply bought into the myth with their ten gallon hats, boots and spurs, and pearl-buttoned yoked shirts. However, the cowboy myth is not without complications when it comes to characterizing male relationships, particularly when interpreted by two emotionally confused Wyoming ranch hands. For Jack, the importance of cowboy mythology to their relationship is captured through a single image remembered of his time on Brokeback, when Ennis had stolen up behind him as he stood in front of the fire and held him in a silent embrace that satisfied some 'shared and sexless hunger':

> They had stood that way for a long time in front of the fire ... The minutes ticked by from the round watch in Ennis's pocket ... Ennis's breath came slow and quiet, he hummed, rocked a little in the sparklight and Jack leaned against the steady heartbeat ... until Ennis, dredging up a rusty but still useable phrase from the childhood time before his mother died, said, "Time to hit the hay, cowboy. I got a go. Come on, you're sleepin on your feet like a horse," and gave Jack a shake, a push, and went off in the darkness. Jack heard his spurs tremble as he mounted, the words "see you tomorrow," and the horse's shuddering snort, grind of hoof on stone.

(pp. 310–11)

This moment casts Jack as a romantic in the mould of F. Scott Fitzgerald's Jay Gatsby, whose relationship with Daisy Buchanan is distilled into the highly sentimental memory of a single kiss taken

on a summer's night. Just as Gatsby's encounter remains sexually
censored, Jack's passion is replaced by a 'shared sexless hunger',
with an anonymous Ennis fulfilling the role of both mother and
lover allowing Jack to return to a childhood dream of being a
cowboy. It is a dream forged in the glimmering of the campfire,
fanned by the breathless rendition of traditional tunes, the
neighing of horses and the tremble of spurs. Through Ennis's
observation 'you're sleepin on your feet like a horse', the narrator
artfully extends the myth that a cowboy's best friend is his horse.
The only sour note in this image of perfect reciprocity is the
presence of the pocket watch, given to Jack by Aguirre. Now in
Ennis's pocket, it acts as a reminder of the world outside Brokeback, where time is work-time. On Brokeback, time is measured by
their humming and gentle rocking, and the steady heartbeat that
counts off their time of happiness together.

For Jack and Ennis, as for Witkin, cowboy dreams are rooted in
childhood fantasy. Both men exist in a state of arrested development. With their childhoods shattered by death and cruel fathers,
cowboy dreams were among the few things that sustained them.
Ennis recalls how his emotionally inarticulate father justified his
violent child-rearing philosophy with the aphoristic 'Nothin like
hurtin' somebody to make him hear good' – and 'hurtin somebody'
is what men do throughout the story (p. 300). In one particular
example, Ennis recounts how as a child he was taken as a warning
to see the mutilated body of a suspected homosexual; the action
proves spectacularly successful, since he grows up as homophobic
as his father. When his parents are killed, the emotionally stunted
young Ennis finds security not with his older brother and sister,
but on the various ranches where he finds himself working: hence
ranch work and performing the role of a cowboy are intimately
connected for Ennis to notions of family life.

Jack too is the product of harsh parenting. In a memory that recalls the young Loyal's treatment at the hands of Mink, and is formative in the development of his sexual identity, Jack relates how as a 3-year-old he was savagely beaten and urinated on by his father for sprinkling on the bathroom floor. Significantly, it is during this event that Jack notices that his father had not been circumcised, his foreskin appearing as an 'anatomical disconformity' to the young boy while 'I seen they'd cut me different like you'd crop a ear or scorch a brand. No way to get it right with him after that' (pp. 314–15). After what, we may ask? In Freudian terms, as the critic Jim Stacy has observed in his essay 'Buried in the Family Plot', Jack perhaps fears the castration that has already been partially achieved – a revelation that will scar him for life; or maybe it is because in that very element that identifies his sexuality he has been treated like a calf. Whichever, it marks him out as different from his father, and his father has seemingly noted a difference in him. Perhaps it is this sense of difference that prevents John C. from sharing any of his bull-riding secrets with Jack, or even coming to see him ride. When Ennis meets him following Jack's death, he recognizes in him 'a not uncommon type with the hard need to be the stud duck in the pond', obsessed with Jack's refusal (he refuses the word son) to be buried in the family plot, which he takes as another sign of his 'difference' (p. 313). His mother, 'careful in her movements as though recovering from an operation', is clearly used to his brutal domination, and used to mediating between them (p. 313). Significantly, she has 'kept his room like it was when he was a boy', its 'narrow boy's bed', a whittled rack and a BB gun a testament to a young man's desire to play at cowboys and Indians (pp. 314–15). Through such fantasies Jack has escaped his father's harsh masculine regime, and yet, as his bull riding indicates, he has remained, like the room, in the midst of these childhood dreams.

It is the mountain itself that allows both characters to live out these childhood fantasies. When Jack parks his pick-up, the characters seem to step back in time: it is 1963, yet there are no vehicles on the mountain, there is no news of the Vietnam War, the assassination of Kennedy, or the Civil Rights movement. Indeed, the only contemporary event mentioned, the sinking of the *Thresher* submarine with the death of all hands in April 1963, simply reinforces the theme of men powerless to avoid their doom as they fall in slow motion (p. 289). On the mountain they can play at being cowboys, sitting around the fire drinking whiskey and telling stories of horses and dogs that they have owned. Jack even plays the harmonica while Ennis, like a latter-day Gene Autry, sings along! The only named song, 'The Strawberry Roan', is, as Patterson has made clear, a humorous cowboy song about a rider who fails in his attempts to master a bucking horse: a song that alludes to the world of Wild West virility that brings them together but warns of inadequacies and looks forward to the trouble that Jack will have mastering Ennis (p. 290).

Beneath their macho posturing, however, Proulx sets out to explore the tension that arises when young men try to live up to the cowboy archetype, a model of masculinity that privileges male relationships above all others, but condemns intimacy among men. Through the narrator's patient cataloguing of a domestic routine in which one cooks and cleans while the other commutes and guards – roles which conform to those of a stereotypical heterosexual family – Proulx demonstrates that the cowboy lifestyle can lead to a blurring of traditional gender relations. Significantly, Ennis and Jack swap jobs – indicating that they feel more comfortable conforming to differently gendered roles to those randomly assigned by Joe Aguirre, with Jack preferring the more 'feminized' role. The continual reinforcement of such roles, the late-night drinking and the feeling of isolation allows their largely wordless romance to develop. And yet, of course, the leap from 'buddies' to sexual partners is profound, not least because of the impact that it has on their perception of themselves as cowboys. Significantly, the terminology that both men employ to describe their behaviour – Jack's climatic 'gun's goin *off*' and his later avowal that it was 'a one-shot thing' – suggests that they are only able to externalize their confused feelings when framed within the language of cowboy mythology (p. 291). The narrator is complicit in these allusions, describing the motel room in which they re-forge their relationship after four years in terms that resemble a barn: 'The room stank of semen and smoke and sweat and whiskey, of old carpet and sour hay, saddle leather, shit and cheap soap' (p. 297). Even Ennis's acknowledgement of the dangers inherent in their relationship – 'there's no reins on this one' – transforms their desire into a wild bucking horse, which, like the 'Strawberry Roan', enhances rather than compromises their perceptions of their masculinity (p. 299).

Home on the range: cowboys and domesticity

Following their descent from Brokeback, it seems that both men are condemned to the life of wandering outcasts: they have strayed from Aguirre's injunction to 'SLEEP WITH THE SHEEP', the narrator observing wryly that when Ennis and Jack's sheep mingle with those of another flock, 'in a disquieting way everything seemed mixed' (pp. 285, 292). The denial of their homosexuality seems hollow; the narrator's apposite double-negative in Ennis's

statement 'I'm not no queer' indicates a confused lack of accep-
tance, while his visceral retching suggests that he is both love-sick
and sickened by his behaviour (pp. 291–3). It would be easy,
therefore, to interpret their subsequent marriages as further
denials combined with an attempt to conform to safer sexual
stereotypes, and the failure of these heterosexual relations as
predictable due to their latent homosexuality. But this is too
simplistic: Ennis, at least, shows no inclination for other men, and
furthermore, although his sex life with Alma recreates that with
the 'bucking horse' Jack, their marriage is not blighted by misogyny. Instead, from the narrator's description, it seems that their
marital breakdown has less to do with Ennis's repressed homosexuality than the incompatibility of domestic life with the cowboy
genre. Initially Ennis is happy enough because he is able to conceive of his family as an extension of ranch work. The family
bedroom at Hi-Top Ranch, for example, is described as 'full of the
smell of old blood and milk and baby shit, and the sounds were of
squalling and sucking and Alma's sleepy groans, all reassuring of
fecundity and life's continuance to one who worked with livestock'
(p. 293). His horse, daughters and Jack – the things he cares most
about in the world – all receive the same endearment 'little darlin',
indicating that Ennis is most content when viewing his life in
terms of cowboy mythology (p. 295). Things go wrong for Ennis
when they move above the laundry, where the tumble of domestic
appliances replaces the whisper of the tumbleweed.

Alma's decision to leave Ennis derives less from her suspicions
concerning his sexuality than from the problems that affect most
families. For Jack, his relationship with Ennis is symbolized by the
memory of their embrace before an open fire on Brokeback;
similarly, Alma's suspicion is reduced to 'the embrace she had
glimpsed' on the stairs outside the apartment, mediated for us

through the narrator's platitudinous, yet tragically inflected statement that 'she has seen what she had seen' (pp. 302, 296). What she had seen is so far beyond her expectations and experience that she is able to delude herself. As Ennis will do later when Jack is killed, she makes use of the 'open space between what [s]he knew and what [s]he tried to believe' to reinterpret events, exercising the kind of mental acrobatics required by all those seeking to deny what they know to be true (p. 318). Her comment to Ennis when arguing about contraception – 'what you like to do don't make too many babies' – suggests that she knows, but her search for evidence, attaching a note to the fishing line in the creal case, indicates her capacity for denial (pp. 302–3). The space allows her to make a go of the marriage, the narrator making it clear that its 'slow corrosion' derives more from Ennis's 'disinclination to step out and have any fun', his limited contributions to childcare (the narrator's deftly inserted observation that 'Alma's mouth twitched' when Ennis claims to love his little girls 'to pieces' indicating her disagreement), and 'his yearning for low-paid, long-houred ranch work' (pp. 296, 302). It is a catalogue of domestic dissatisfaction that we may imagine delivered in what Ennis calls 'her misery voice' – suggesting that he hears it often (p. 296).

Jack's descent after Brokeback, reported to us in fragments, is more extreme. He lives out his cowboy fantasies by rodeo, an almost self-conscious exhibition of cowboy mythology. Furthermore, his marriage to Lureen, one of its practitioners, offers an acceptable feminized form of the cowboy myth. The marriage founders, however, on his increasing marginalization from the business. His father-in-law (whose farming machinery business represents everything that the cowboy dream refutes) dislikes Jack and, if Jack is to be believed, is willing to pay him handsomely to get rid of him. Like John C. Twist, he clearly senses something different in the behaviour of Jack that does not equate with his idea of what a man, and particularly a son-in-law, should be. After his death, Lureen proves herself to be the one who has the head for business, reducing Jack to a vague managerial capacity. As on Brokeback, it is Jack who falls into the 'feminized role', worrying about his son's schooling while 'Lureen ha[s] the money and call[s] the shots' (p. 307). As the sound of the rodeo gives way to the image of Lureen behind a desk with a calculator, we are reminded of the domestic imprisonment of both men.

A pastoral tragedy

Escape for the two men comes in the form of fishing and hunting trips, activities that enable them to fulfil their relationship against a backdrop that is part of the mythology of American masculinity. Significantly, they do not return to Brokeback, not wishing to sully its symbolic importance by making it the venue of a few 'high-altitude fucks' (p. 309). Instead the narrator compresses their relationship into a travelogue in which they work through a land-scape – 'the Big Horns, Medicine Bows ... Owl Creeks, the Bridger-Teton Range ...' – which evokes the spirit of the Wild West (p. 304). Such male bonding in the Great Outdoors is typical of Hemingway, especially during his 'men without women' phase. His *The Sun also Rises* (1926) is of particular interest since it describes a scene in which the central protagonists escape from the female-dominated Paris salons to go fishing in the mountains. At one point Bill Gorton says to Jake Barnes (who carries a more violent version of the sexual wound that marks Jack): 'Listen. You're a hell of a good guy, and I'm fonder of you than anybody on earth. I couldn't tell you that in New York. It'd mean I was a faggot.' The denial of homosexuality is implicit in the use of the conditional, yet there is also an acknowledgement that the codes of masculinity change once they get away from civilization and into the mountains. The fishing trips of Jack and Ennis provide the same emotional realignment. Ennis's coarse admission to Jack that 'I never had no thoughts a doin it with another guy except I sure wrang it out a hundred times thinkin about you', simply offers a cruder more explicit exploration of the confusion in heterosexual relations that can take place away from more restrictive social mores (p. 298).

Despite Jack's desire to consolidate their love in a more long-term relationship, Ennis refuses, citing familial responsibilities and the fear of persecution. More pertinently, however, he remains in denial about his homosexuality right to the end. Thus, the ferocity of his assault upon Jack for his euphemistic visits to Mexico during the climatic final parting is fuelled not only by jealousy, but also by the fear that an acknowledgement of Jack's sexual orientation would entail his own. As an exasperated Jack claims: 'We could a had a real good life together, a fuckin real good life. You wouldn't do it, Ennis, so what we got now is Brokeback Mountain' (p. 309). Since the story concludes in the 1980s, their relationship could indeed have ended differently, if they had moved to the city, Mexico, anywhere where there were no cowboys. But for Ennis this is impossible, since his relationship with Jack can only be sanctified when viewed through the prism of cowboy nostalgia and the Great Outdoors. Without the elevating dream of Brokeback, he is left having to admit the truth of his own sexual nature.

Proulx recalls that 'while I was working on this story, I was occasionally close to tears. I felt guilty that their lives were so difficult, yet there was nothing I could do about it. It couldn't end any other way.' To many gay critics, however, this simply panders to the cliché that homosexual love must end badly. Why, asks the critic W. C. Harris (Stacy), does she leave Ennis to shuffle around his trailer alone, in fear of his sexuality? Why couldn't Jack end up living a fulfilled homosexual life with a new partner in New Mexico, like Tom Outland and Roddy Blake in Willa Cather's *The Professor's House* (1925)? It is a valid criticism, but such an end is more befitting of a realist drama than the modern tragedy that Proulx has in mind. Furthermore, it would also deny the opportunity to explore the complex reactions to his death articulated by Lureen and Ennis, reactions which explore further how individuals use the 'open space' between knowledge and belief to forge their own narratives.

Lureen's phone conversation with Ennis sanitizes the mystery of Jack's death for both herself and the world at large, presenting a story, which may or may not be true, and which she may or may not believe, to a character who she may or may not suspect to be her husband's lover. Significantly, we do not hear her account directly; it is reported through the narrator from Ennis's perspective, the detail of her 'level voice' suggesting that she is parroting an account given to her. Even when we hear her voice, we are guided in our response by Ennis's observation that 'she was polite but the little voice was cold as snow' – the tone of somebody who is masking a public disgrace rather than mourning a loved one. Ironically, her reference to Brokeback as the place 'where the bluebirds sing and there's a whiskey spring', to indicate Jack's propensity for delusion, merely underlines her own. The words are, as Patterson has noted, taken from the old hobo song 'Big Rock Candy Mountain' made popular by Burl Ives, which tells of an earthly paradise where the hobos are happy together. However, in the original version the male relationships are far more intimate, suggesting that Lureen, like Ives, is happier with a cleaner version of events. For Ennis, however, Jack's death can only be interpreted as the result of homophobia, symbolized by the 'tire iron'. It is, tragically, a fulfilment of Ennis's father's warning, and therefore a justification for his former refusal to live together. The threat of violence was always present for Ennis; thus in dreams that take him back to the most idealized moments on Brokeback, the spoon handle sticking out of the can of beans that they share 'was the kind that could be used as a tire iron' – beans, the humble staple of the cowboy's campfire diet (p. 318).

The shirts, by contrast, become a symbol of their repressed love, the memory of Hylas clasped by the heroic Hercules. They are first mentioned in the prologue: 'The shirts hanging on a nail shudder slightly', the intransitive verb 'shudder' implying both sexual excitement and fear – an apt description of their relationship (p. 283). However, it is only when Ennis discovers them in the closet within a closet (an obvious symbol of repression) within Jack's childishly furnished bedroom that their significance is explained. They are described 'like two skins, one inside the other, two in one' covered in the blood of their final encounter (p. 316). The blood is both a symbol of their parting grief, their hatred for what each has revealed about the other, and also, as the critic John Kitterman has observed, their blood brotherhood in the American mythos (Stacy). Noticeably, Jack's shirt enfolds Ennis's, a reversal of their positions in the symbolic flashback scene around the campfire on Brokeback; Jack therefore has come to consider himself the protector of the emotionally vulnerable Ennis. Furthermore, it is only through the substitute of the shirts that Ennis, with Jack now dead, is prepared to embrace him, pressing his face into the fabric while trying to summon up the memory of his earlier embrace of him on Brokeback Mountain (p. 316).

It is entirely appropriate that the shirts and a postcard of Brokeback Mountain should make up the shrine to Jack in Ennis's trailer, since postcards have been used throughout as a means of arranging their assignations. This ensemble is not tucked away in a closet, and when Ennis steps back and begins 'Jack, I swear—', his elliptical sentence allows us to speculate on his feelings (p. 317). The phrasing echoes the marriage vows, suggesting that, given another chance, Ennis would be ready to step out of the closet and embrace his sexuality with Jack. This, however, is immediately undermined by the narrator's bathetic observation that 'Jack had never asked him to swear anything and was himself not the swearing kind' (p. 317). Furthermore, the fact that it remains one of those unfinished sentences that pepper Ennis's speech patterns, reminding us of his inability to even say the word homosexual, suggests that in his mind his 'marriage' to Jack remains within the confines of the trailer and his imagination.

4

The Novel's Reception

Postcards met with almost immediate critical acclaim, with David Bradley asserting in the *New York Times* that Proulx has 'come close' to writing the Great American Novel – that is, a novel that offers a panoramic meditation on American geography, history, social make-up and culture. She was awarded the 13th PEN/Faulkner Award for Fiction, the first time for a female author. This singularity led some critics to suspect the panel of being swayed by political correctness, fears to which Proulx herself was not immune. When pressed on the matter by Esther Fein in the *New York Times*, she admitted: 'Being the first woman does give winning this a whole other dimension'; a statement later qualified by her admission to David Streitfield in the *Washington Post* that 'I'm telling myself it's the book that's valued, not the fact that a woman wrote it ... a book doesn't really have a sex at all.' Hoping to dispel such charges, one of the judges, Frederick Busch, claimed: 'It's safe to say there was no political agenda going on ... I became a fan the first time I read *Postcards*.'

What most excited critics was Proulx's breadth of vision combined with her innovative prose. In the *Sunday Telegraph*, Lucasta Miller commended Proulx for the vastness of her landscapes, the length of her time-span, and the eclectic nature of her characters, concluding that the novel 'sets itself up as the elusive, proverbial "Great American Novel"'. Other British critics sought parallels among the American greats, thereby aligning her with a tradition that is both unashamedly masculine and, to some degree, old fashioned. Shena Mackay in the *Independent on Sunday* drew parallels with Faulkner, while the *Daily Telegraph* noted that 'not since Steinbeck has the migrant worker's life been so evocatively rendered'. Zachery Leader, reviewing the novel in *The Times Literary Supplement*, made more specific links between Loyal's tragedy and those explored in the works of Naturalist writers such as Richard Wright's *Native Son* and Theodore Dreiser's *An American Tragedy*. This theme was taken up by Bradley, who argued that the novel is indeed 'a true American tragedy' in which 'the consequences of Loyal's transgression are visited upon unnumbered generations'. This, of course, taps into the oldest of literary traditions, in which Loyal as both farmer and trapper is transformed into both Cain and Abel; Dub into a prodigal son and a one-handed Esau; and Mink into an Old Testament patriarch.

While praising her breadth of vision, a number of critics took issue with the sprawling, fragmentary nature of her narrative, a legacy, Tom Shone claimed in *The Sunday Times*, of her background as a short story writer. Leader argued that Proulx's tendency toward 'terrific set piece descriptions' came at the expense of the gradual unfolding of broader themes which would have given 'the narrative some final, or at least clearer, shape and meaning'. Sabine Durant was less conciliatory in the *Independent*, arguing that 'the plot courts confusion: there are huge leaps of time, incidents are signposted important then dropped [and] subjects' names are sometimes kept back for several pages'. Bradley, however, defended the fragmentary nature of the narrative, pointing out that the postcards themselves 'transform a rambling tale into a minimalist saga'. This view was shared by Shone, who not only commended Proulx's bravery in attempting a 'pocket-sized', or 'postcard-sized', epistolary novel on her debut, but also acknowledged that the postcards prevent the novel from becoming a 'domino trail of disconnected disasters'. He likens the novel's structure to a 'Hockney Polaroid collage' in which each photograph offers a slightly different view which both complements and collides with its neighbour to form 'something much more than the sum of the snapshots'.

'Story makes this novel compelling; technique makes it beautiful,' Bradley asserted in his review, and gave as example such innovations as the 'What I see' sections, which he praised as 'lyrical, naturalistic elegies ... in which she captures the rhythms of a nation'. Most American critics echoed these sentiments; Patti Doten in the *Boston Globe* praised the novel's 'powerful, sensual language', while Frederick Busch claimed in the *Chicago Tribune* that it is written in 'a language that demands to be lingered over – for the pungent bite of its effect and for the pleasure of learning how good, and even gorgeous, sentences are written'. The generally more circumspect British reviewers, however, remained deaf to Proulx's 'rhythms'. Leader, for example, was impressed by the novel as a whole, but not the compressed sentences and stacked metaphors, which, he felt, left it 'crowded on the level of the sentence' and 'often overwritten'. Similarly, James Walton's otherwise effusive review in the *Daily Telegraph* was qualified by his arch observation that the novel occasionally slides into 'clichés of the Trailer Park school of fiction (very short sentences. Without verbs. Full stops. For no apparent reason.), and sometimes runs aground on the rocks of relentless nautical metaphor'.

It was left to Henry Porter in the *Guardian* to take issue with the stance of his critical colleagues, who, he implies, have failed to keep pace with cultural shifts. American writers, he argues, use language that 'crackles with electricity'. Its 'lack of clausal form-ality' and 'present tense terseness' seem appropriate to 'describe the world in the late 20th century'. By contrast, the English prose tradition appears to be 'trapped in an age of gentility'.

5

The Story's Reception

The story's original publication in *The New Yorker* magazine was greeted with immediate critical acclaim, helping the magazine to win the US National Magazine Awards in 1998. It also won an O. Henry Prize (an annual award for short stories of exceptional merit) and was included in its annual collection. This success convinced Proulx's British publisher – Fourth Estate – to bring the story out in a slim volume. Her British editor, Christopher Potter, recalls Proulx arriving in Britain to sit as one of the judges for the Orange Prize for female fiction and giving him a copy of the story which she claimed was 'the best thing that I have ever written'. Potter agreed, quickly transforming the 10,000-word story into a novella, which immediately entered the top ten fiction paperbacks list in Britain and sparked a debate on the revival of the short story as the perfect medium for the time-poor urban sophisticate.

Its publication history means that the earliest considered critical response to the story came from British reviewers. Despite its dismally unpromising title, Vanessa Thorpe's 'Ranch hands get raunchy' in the *Independent on Sunday* offered a thoughtful engagement with the text, which praised Proulx's 'emotional restraint and lack of sentimentality'. In *The Times Literary Supplement* Lucy Atkins argued that 'Proulx's strongest traits – linguistic economy, lyricism, an awareness of the nuances and brutality of relationships – are compressed into a single moving and expansive work: at once a tragic love story, a hymn to the wild spaces of Wyoming, a lament against the strictures of society and a challenging exploration of masculinity.'

The bulk of the reviews, however, appeared following the story's inclusion in the collection *Close Range*. Most critics – including Will Eaves in *The Times Literary Supplement* and Christopher Lehmann-Haupt in *The New York Times* – considered *Brokeback Mountain* 'the volume's strongest story', and the academic Elaine Showalter, no less, described it as 'The most startling and sensational of the stories', for which Proulx was her 'choice for the artist of the year' and 'candidate for the new woman of the millennium'. (Interestingly, for the writers Garrison Keillor and John Updike it was 'The Half Skinned Steer' – with its complex series of narrative voices and time shifts – that drew special praise, the latter anthologizing it in his *The Best American Short Stories of the Century*.) For many critics, the collection, and *Brokeback Mountain* in particular, was important because is successfully debunked the old myths of the American West. Proulx herself explained that the stories were designed to be 'a backhand swipe at the mythology of the West – the old beliefs that aren't really true, like the idea that there are no homosexuals in Wyoming'. Mary Flanagan, writing in the *Independent*, claimed she had succeeded in dispelling the glamour of the anarchic cowboy, something that McCarthy, for all his grittiness, has proved unable to do. Gail Caldwell was more forthright in the *Boston Sunday Globe*, arguing that *Brokeback*

Mountain 'does some of the best things a story can do. It abolishes the old West clichés, excavates and honours a certain kind of elusive life, then nearly levels with you with the emotional weight at its centre.'

Many critics felt that *Brokeback Mountain* offered a departure from the usual Proulx style, in which character is so often subservient to plot. In Jack and Ennis she had created characters with real psychological depth and an interior life that distanced them from their natural environment. Interestingly, Proulx herself recalls that when writing the story Jack and Ennis 'did something that, as a writer, I had never experienced before – they began to become very damn real'. Clare Messud, reviewing in the *Guardian*, was clearly in agreement, arguing that the story demonstrates that 'Proulx is able, when she chooses, to engage as much with her characters as with their surroundings; and that when she does so ... she is more than an impressive stylist; she is an exceptional writer.' It is a view echoed by Richard Eder in *The New York Times*, who argued that *Brokeback Mountain* 'demonstrates her extraordinary insight into males', whether she is describing their bodies or 'the roughness and wary companionship of a raw macho society'. However, Michele Roberts, reviewing the collection in the *Independent on Sunday*, was of a different opinion, arguing that Proulx had become enthralled with a world of 'rugged, tight-lipped masculinity' to such a degree that Jack and Ennis are not even allowed to make love to each other without an excess of manly squalor.

In her early review, Lucy Atkins had praised 'Proulx's linguistic precision' in the story, arguing that it is 'less self-conscious than her previous works', but remarkably effective. Her judgement is widely echoed by subsequent critics, Caldwell adopting a musical analogy in her assertion that 'some of the ferocious impact of

Proulx's writing comes from her precision of form, a free-fall confident as a jazz saxophonist'. Both Eder in *The New York Times* and Will Eaves in *The Times Literary Supplement* praised Proulx for her restraint, the former noting that her prose is 'violent and impacted and mastered just at the point where, having gone all the way to the edge, it is about to go over'. Eaves, much like Atkins before him, felt that *Brokeback Mountain* was 'technically perfect', focusing in particular on the way in which the 'tension between its percussive descriptions and strangled conversations shows how the clearly seen must often (in art as in life) go unsaid'.

Those things 'left unsaid' certainly characterized the reception of the story within the gay community, which responded, as Proulx noted in an interview with Sandy Cohen of the *Associated Press*, 'with a deafening silence'. While acknowledging her surprise she recalled that what she received instead:

Were letters from individuals, gay people, some of them absolutely heartbreaking. And over the years, those letters have continued and certainly are continuing now. Some of them are extremely fine, people who write and say, "This is my story. This is why I left Idaho, Wyoming, Iowa." Perhaps the most touching ones are from fathers, who say, "Now I understand the kind of hell my son went through." It's enormously wonderful to know that you've touched people, that you've truly moved them.

Perhaps this is the most valuable aspect of the reception of the story, and would have made a fitting conclusion, were it not for Proulx's most recent admission to Susan Salter Reynolds in the *Los Angeles Times* that she wished she had never written the story, such has been its misappropriation by readers who have continued to send her rewrites. They seem determined, she observes elsewhere, to 'correct what they see as an unbearably disappointing story. ... They certainly don't get the message that if you can't fix it, you've got to stand it.'

Few critics mentioned the possibility of a film, presumably because few thought that it would ever be made. Even Proulx, when requested for a film option, found herself wondering 'what producers would be interested in a story about homophobic gay Wyoming ranch hands? What actors would have the guts to do this? What director would take the risk?' So, how did a film that challenges centuries of Western mythology while undermining that quintessential symbol of American masculinity, the cowboy, come to be made?

6

The Story's Performance

From story to screenplay

In her essay 'Climbing Brokeback Mountain' published in *Brokeback Mountain: Story to Screenplay*, Diana Ossana, half of the writing team responsible for the screenplay of the film, recalls how she came upon Proulx's story in *The New Yorker* during a bout of insomnia: 'I was seduced by the simple lyricism of Annie's prose and then startled by its rawness and power ... I felt, to paraphrase Annie's own words, as if my guts had been pulled out hand over hand a yard at a time.' In the morning she asked her writing partner, Larry McMurtry (author of the *Lonesome Dove* Western series) to read it, and he recognized immediately that here was a cowboy story that had been sitting for years waiting to be told. They phoned their manager and outlined the plot, but he advised them to forget it because a film 'would never get made'. However, he agreed to read the story anyway; by the end of the day he had phoned them back urging them to contact Proulx immediately.

It took three months to write the screenplay, Ossana noting that, unlike most adaptations, which involve editing and compression, with *Brokeback Mountain* the onus was on 'rounding out the characters, creating new scenes, fleshing out existing ones'. They sent the finished script to various producers, but nobody would touch it; instead it quickly gained the unenviable label in Hollywood circles of the 'gay cowboy story'. Ironically, as Proulx recalls, the small independent directors who did take an interest were part of an Art-House Metropolitan-scene that simply did not understand the rural West. When Focus Features came forward and suggested the Taiwanese-born Ang Lee (who had recently recreated *The Hulk*) as a possible director, Proulx was incredulous. The location of their initial meeting, a chic New York bar, seemed to confirm her doubts, but Proulx recalls that his quietly spoken manner and the confession that he 'had recently lost his father' prompted her to hope that he might use his sorrow and sense of loss creatively.

After nearly seven years the film went into production, on a tight budget, in and around Calgary, Alberta in late spring of 2004. Proulx kept at a distance, but when she found out that Lee intended to shift the scene in which Jack and Ennis lay out their lives in the Motel Siesta and meld it with their climactic final meeting, she immediately wrote to him pleading for its restoration to the central scene of the story. When he would not change it, she acknowledged, 'it was out of my hands, no longer my story, but Ang Lee's film'. The filming took six months, with a further year in post-production, after which Proulx was able to watch the finished product at a private screening. She was dumbfounded, recalling how she felt that the crew 'had gotten into my mind and pulled out the images'. Interestingly, she conceded that she could understand the power and timing of Lee's alteration of the motel scene. In an ultimate tribute she noted: 'Here it was, the point that writers do not like to admit; in our time film can be more powerful than the written word ... my story was not mangled but enlarged into huge and gripping imagery that rattled minds and squeezed hearts.'

The film

Ossana argues that 'the film stands faithfully beside *Brokeback Mountain* the story', which in so many ways it does: much of the dialogue and many of the screen directions are lifted straight from the story. Certainly, Proulx's fears that Lee would give short shrift to the presentation of the mountain itself, thereby losing 'the literal grounding of the story', proved unfounded, as Rodrigo Prieto (the director of photography) produced sweeping panoramas of rivers of sheep which dominate the opening sequences. Indeed, Lee seems keen to accentuate the Arcadian imagery, adding scenes of Ennis carrying a lamb in a saddle bag, and Jack fording a brook with a sheep on his shoulder: they are protectors and nurturers in this idyllic surrounding – heirs to the tradition of Theocritus. Like Proulx, and much to the consternation of some critics, Lee also spends a great deal of time establishing the camp routine in order to develop the psychological intimacy between Jack and Ennis before their first sexual encounter. Two additional scenes help in this process: when Ennis' horse is spooked by a black bear it leads to a familiar heterosexual domestic encounter. Initially an impatient Jack, waiting at the camp, is angry that his food isn't 'on the table', but when he notices the injury his mood alters; he unthinkingly takes off his bandana and raises it to Ennis's forehead. Ossana's direction reads: 'Jack hesitates ... awkward ...

hands the bandana to Ennis', a moment of instinctive tenderness brought under control at the last minute. In the very next scene, also additional, they are shooting a deer together – bonding in a reassuringly masculine manner.

The separation of the pastoral innocence of Brokeback from the domestic lives of both men remains as pronounced in the film as the story, and yet a number of additional scenes have the effect of subtly transforming the dynamic of their heterosexual relations. In Proulx's story, Ennis's marriage to Alma is dismissed in a couple of paragraphs as little more than time away from Jack. The film presents them as a happy couple, sledging ('Alma squeals in delight; Ennis whoops it up') and enjoying a drive-in movie ('Ennis has him arm round her; she's pregnant, just showing'). When the girls are born, domestic life is presented as difficult, but Ennis is a less cynical and more caring father figure. Indeed, both men are portrayed as better fathers in the film; Ennis remains loved by his daughters even after the divorce, and Jack is pictured teaching his son to drive a tractor – 'whoa, son, there you go. No hands!' – in a scene of typical male bonding. The effect of these additional scenes is to suggest that Ennis adapts to heterosexual domesticity with relative success. As he stands, cowboy hat on head, silhouetted against the Fourth of July fireworks having dispatched two foul-mouthed bikers, he appears to embody all the masculine virtues of the cowboy mythology: a brooding man of few words who is prepared to leap to the defence of his family with actions rather than words. It is, of course, a scene full of irony, since, in the very act of defending his family, Ennis demonstrates the characteristics that will undermine it. Not only does domesticity sit uneasily with traditional cowboy mythology, but the revelation that 'pardners' can become more intimate than expected is a direct challenge to the family.

Jack's life during the four years apart allows the film to explore the more feminized male. In the story Ennis wonders whether 'you ever get the feeling, I don't know, when you're in town, and someone looks at you, suspicious . . . like he *knows*'. In Jack's case, men seem to 'know', which the film uses to dramatize the dangers of rural homophobia. In an additional scene where Jack attempts to buy a drink for a rodeo clown who had earlier saved him from a mauling, Ossana's screen direction notes: 'There is something, a frisson, a vibe, that gives the clown an uneasy feeling . . .' When he joins a group of drinkers, he shares something that makes them all stare over at Jack, who realizes he had better leave. In the film, therefore, Jack's marriage is presented as a bid for heterosexual and financial security as much as a consequence of love. Yet even here Jack is presented in a more 'feminine' role, as it is Lureen who seduces him and ends up on top in their first sexual encounter in the car. In marriage, his inability to conform to the narrow definition of masculinity is dangerous, a feature dramatized by Ossana through her creation of Jack's father-in-law, L.D. A replacement 'stud duck' for both Aguirre and John C. Twist in Jack's development, he seems to *know* about Jack, continually undermining the younger man's role as both husband and father. When Bobby is born, it is L.D. who is pictured with the radiant mother, dismissing Jack from the reproductive process with his cooing 'isn't he the spittin' image of his grandpa', and also, more practically, from the family group to fetch the formula milk from the car. As he tosses him the keys, the scene echoes that experienced in Aguirre's trailer: like Ennis, he isn't worth the reach. Later in the film, L.D.'s contempt for Jack's effeminate behaviour is made clear in his insistence that Bobby watches the football during the Thanksgiving supper: 'You want your son to grow up to be a man don't you, daughter? (*direct look at Jack*) Boys should watch football.'

The effect of these additions is to alter the relationship of Jack and Ennis when they meet again. The critic Lisa Arellano has gone so far as to argue that to some extent Jack is transformed into the 'Jack Nasty' that Alma identifies, the predatory homosexual breaking up a reasonably stable family unit (Stacy). But this does not seem to be the film's intention; Jack is not depicted unfavourably, he is not a predatory male, but rather a blast of fresh air from Brokeback – a quality that Lee emphasizes through the addition of the amplified sound of wind blowing during the kiss observed by Alma. In fact, the film goes out of its way to present their relationship as a return to pastoral innocence (the reason for Lee's cutting of the long, seedy scene in the Phoenix motel becomes apparent). Scenes of the two of them splashing around in lakes and mountain riding ('like Randolph Scott and Joel McCrea in *Ride the High Country*', as the screen direction notes) are contrasted with domestic scenes, which become increasingly cramped and unhappy. Even their lovemaking, which is rough and ready in Proulx's story, is, as Patterson has noted, depicted through soft focus shots of burnished bodies and scenes of simple tenderness in which they lie in each others arms.

Lee further emphasizes their happiness together through the contrast with heterosexual couplings which remain largely dysfunctional: the corrosion of Alma and Ennis' relationship derives as much from the weight of childcare and the anaesthetic of television as his sexuality. His relationship with Cassie is half-hearted, their drunken daytime dancing in seedy bars, initiated by her invitation 'C'mon cowboy, you're stayin' on your feet', offers a parody of the single idealized moment that symbolizes his love for Jack. Lureen ages gracelessly, her big hair and heavy make-up failing to hide the hard, chain-smoking businesswoman – truly she is her father's child. L.D. and John C. Twist are presented as bullies who have successfully terrorized their own wives into submission. Frankly, we fear for Alma Jr's marriage to Kurt, a redneck whose gaudy Chevy Camaro is a vulgar assertion of his masculinity. Alma's second husband, Monroe, offers a glimpse of the new man, but the way he primly slices the Thanksgiving turkey with his electric carver while smiling smugly at Ennis almost makes us nostalgic for L.D.'s insistence that the 'stud duck does the carvin''. Most damning of all are Jack and Lureen's friends the Malones, as Lashawn's vacuous chattering drives her husband to propose to Jack that they escape to a cabin where they can 'drink a little whiskey, fish some. Get away, you know?' Jack does know, and the film's message is disturbingly clear: domesticity and dominant women drive men to rediscover their masculinity in the woods, with sometimes surprising consequences.

Considering the short shrift that heterosexual relations receive in the film, it is perhaps surprising that Jack is continually attempting to replicate them in his dream of a 'little cow-and-calf operation' with Ennis. In the story we are guided to believe that Ennis's refusal derives less from the pragmatic reasons he gives – the threat of violence and his need to support his daughters – than his internalized homophobia. In the film this alters, as the risk of extreme homophobic aggression and Ennis's affection for his daughters are continually emphasized. For example, instead of Ennis telling Jack about his father showing him the mutilated corpse of the homosexual cowboy, we are shown the body as seen through the eyes of Ennis before, according to Ossana's screen direction, 'WE SEE the horror wash over his 9-year-old face.' Following Alma's accusations at the Thanksgiving supper, the narrator alludes to Ennis having a 'short grubby fight' in a bar; in the film this is transformed into Ennis being repeatedly punched by a 'roughneck the size of a bear' – the kind of beating that he will receive if Alma's suspicions become public. Most significantly, it is Ennis's interpretation, that Jack was clubbed to death with a 'tire iron', that is graphically depicted over Lureen's account of events.

Ennis's daughters play little part in Proulx's story, but in the film they are reintroduced at various stages of their development. Furthermore, it is clear that their presence is not simply designed to remind the viewer of Ennis's familial duty, rather there is a great deal of reciprocated affection, captured by one of Ossana's directions during the Thanksgiving supper with Monroe: 'His girls love him, their faces rapt when their daddy speaks.' By contrast, Bobby is a miniature L.D. The film emphasizes these new priorities – the external hostility combined with the emotional importance of Ennis's daughters – in an additional scene following Ennis's divorce. When Jack turns up unexpectedly at Ennis's isolated line cabin to offer himself as a replacement, Alma Jr and Jenny are present and offer direct competition for the distraught Jack. Lee also adds the detail of a passing car, which slows down and draws an anxious glance from Ennis – a suggestion of the violent threat that he believes they face. Thus, whereas in the story we are led to feel that Ennis is overly constrained by his fears, in the film it is Jack who is too cavalier with regard to the risks, something dramatized by the onscreen representation of his trip to Mexico.

Ennis can neither play happy families nor go to Mexico, which leaves him isolated and alone in his trailer at the end of both the story and the film. There are, however, a number of additional details in the latter that suggest a happy ending absent from Proulx's original conception. When Alma Jr turns up to ask Ennis to attend her wedding he offers his stock response, an echo of his final excuse for not meeting with Jack: 'Supposed to be on a roundup over near the Tetons.' Whereas he proved inflexible with Jack, her disappointment leads to a new resolution: 'I reckon they can find themselves another cowboy ... my little girl ... is gettin' married.' Familial duty and affection at last conquer the spirit of the cowboy, celebrated with cheap white wine left by Cassie, a reminder of his own failed heterosexual relationship. As she drives away, he notices that she has left a jumper behind and goes to put it in his wardrobe. Here inside the closet, beneath the postcard of Brokeback, are the shirts, the shrine to his male lover. Significantly, the shirts are the other way around to those in the story, with Ennis's now figuratively clutching Jack, suggesting that in death he is prepared to acknowledge his love. It is noticeable, however, that the shirts remain shut away in the closet, and when, as the critic Roy Grundmann has observed, Ennis steps back with his elliptical 'Jack, I swear', it is clearly, in the context of his daughter's wedding, an enactment of his own secret marriage (Stacy). As the camera then pans to the straight road outside the trailer window, the symbolism becomes apparent: he remains wedded to Jack in secret but is determined to travel the straight road, starting with the ultimate symbol of familial and heterosexual love, his daughter's wedding. Ennis, above all others, knows from the death of those he has loved – his parents and Jack – the dangers of deviation from the straight road.

The film's reception

During one of its preview screenings, James Schamus, the film's Executive Producer, recalls with some amusement that 'my wife came out of the ladies' room and said, "There are 15 women in there, and they're all crying." I said, "You ought to see the men's room." ' Clearly the film had hit a nerve. On both sides of the Atlantic, film critics were unanimous in urging audiences to see the film: Philip French of the *Observer* and Stephen Holden in *The New Yorker* described it as a 'moving' and 'majestic' tragedy, while Rick Moody in the *Guardian* went so far as to draw parallels with *Romeo and Juliet*, arguing that it was a 'civic duty' for viewers to wrestle with the themes raised. This critical acclaim was matched by success at numerous award ceremonies, culminating in a Golden Lion for Lee at Venice, a sheaf of awards at the Baftas, and the award for Best Picture at the 63rd Golden Globes (awarded by the Hollywood Foreign Press Association). However, it failed to go on to secure the Oscar for Best Picture, which, as the critic Charles Eliot Mehler has demonstrated in his essay '*Brokeback Mountain* at the Oscars' (Stacy), is highly unusual.

Proulx's anger at the Conservatism of the Academy stopped short of the accusation of homophobia, but her mistrust is clear. But perhaps this is too simple, for, as Mehler has argued, Hollywood's record concerning gay rights is not bad: as early as 1985, the independent film *Kiss of the Spiderwoman*, which concerned the relationship between a political prisoner and his effeminate cellmate, was nominated for a number of Oscars; in 2005 Felicity Huffmann was awarded best actress for her role as a transsexual in the film *Transamerica*; and, most revealingly, in the same year that *Brokeback Mountain* failed to achieve Best Picture, Philip Seymour Hoffman was awarded Best Actor for his depiction of the outrageously camp author Truman Capote in the film of that name. But this is rather the point – Hollywood likes to deal with sexual difference as significantly and safely *different*; *Capote* was acceptable because the writer's prancing exotic manner fell just short of parody; *Brokeback Mountain* violated this fundamental rule by presenting two ordinary men who just happened to be sexually attracted to one another. Ironically, their very ordinariness also offended many gay critics, who objected to the way in which the film had gone through a process of 'hetero-normalization' to reach a wider audience. This included the marketing of the film as a 'universal love story' and the choreographing of photo-shoots in which the male actors were partnered with their stage wives. Effectively, the film succeeded in alienating both groups – leading to the debacle of Oscar night.

7

Further Reading and Discussion Questions

Discussion questions

The following questions are designed to help you explore further your ideas about the story, book and film.

Postcards

1. Proulx incorporates a number of innovations in this novel. How successful are the postcards as a means of structuring the narrative and revealing character? How effective are the 'What I See' sections?

2. Frederick Busch claimed in the *Chicago Tribune* that Proulx's language 'demands to be lingered over – for the pungent bite of its effect and for the pleasure of learning how good, and even gorgeous, sentences are written'. However, James Walton accused Proulx in the *Telegraph* of using 'clichés of the Trailer Park school of fiction (very short sentences. Without verbs. Full stops. For no apparent reason.) ...' Which comes closest to your reading of the

novel? How can you reconcile these differences? Do you think that the nationality of the critics is important?

3. Reviewing the novel in *The New York Times* the critic David Bradley claimed that the novel was a 'true American tragedy' in which 'the consequences of Loyal's transgression are visited upon unnumbered generations'. How responsible is Loyal for the disasters that beset the Blood family?

4. How does Proulx's employment of Classical and Biblical symbols and motifs enrich our reading of the story?

5. 'For me,' Proulx argues, 'the story falls out of place, its geology and climate, the flora, fauna, prevailing winds, the weather.' How important is the landscape in the novel?

6. Much of Proulx's fiction concerns itself with the impact of modernization and outsiders upon a rural environment. Consider this trend in the light of the observations made by Jewell, and the introduction of 'urban bumpkins' such as Witkin.

7. The novel spans a period of history (the 40 years following the Second World War) in which the lives of women changed rapidly. How does the novel reflect these changes?

8. Men seem troubled in the novel: the older generation comprises violent, drunken patriarchs, while the modern generation seems to have lost its way. Consider Proulx's presentation of characters such as Mink, Dub, Ray MacWay and Ben Rainwater.

Brokeback Mountain

1. During their climatic final meeting, an exasperated Jack claims: 'We could a had a real good life together, a fuckin' real good life. You wouldn't do it, Ennis, so what we got now is Brokeback Mountain.' Discuss the importance of Brokeback Mountain in the story. Could they have had a real good life? What prevents them from settling down together?

2. How does Proulx's employment of Classical and Biblical symbols and motifs enrich our reading of the story?

3. Why is it important that, as Proulx has noted, Jack and Ennis 'wanted to be cowboys – part of the great Western myth'?

4. How important are their 'stud duck' fathers in the upbringing of both Jack and Ennis?

5. Proulx recalls that the story 'couldn't end any other way'. Is this true?

6. Although we are moved by their love for each other, Ennis and Jack remain utterly self-absorbed, wreaking havoc on all who come into contact with them – particularly their wives and family. To what extent are we guided to sympathize with the wrong victims in the story?

7. Diana Ossana argues that 'the film stands faithfully beside *Brokeback Mountain* the story'. A number of gay critics, however, have argued that the film succeeds in 'straightening' it out. What do you think?

8. The film introduces some bold new scenes and characters. Consider what the following adds to your interpretation of the story: the Fourth of July picnic during which Ennis dispatches two foul-mouthed bikers; the character of L.D. (particularly at the bedside after the birth of Bobby, and at the Thanksgiving supper); the reintroduction of Ennis's grown-up daughters; the role of Cassie.

Suggestions for further reading

Books by Proulx (listed in order of publication, but with editions used in this book)
Heart Songs (1988), London, New York: Harper Perennial, 2006.
Postcards (1992), London: Fourth Estate, 2003.

The Shipping News (1993), London: Fourth Estate, 1994.
Accordion Crimes (1996), London, New York: Harper Perennial, 2006.
Close Range (1999), London, New York: Harper Perennial, 2006.
That Old Ace in the Hole (2002), London, New York: Harper Perennial, 2004.
Bad Dirt (2004), London, New York: Harper Perennial, 2005.
Fine Just the Way it Is (2008), London: Fourth Estate, 2008.

Articles by Proulx

'Books on Top', *The New York Times*, 26 May 1994.
'Urban Bumpkins', *Washington Post*, 25 September 1994.
'Tell it Like a Person', *Observer*, 15 June 1997.
'How the West was Spun', *Guardian*, 25 June 2005.
Brokeback Mountain: Story to Screenplay, Scribner, New York, London, 2005 (Proulx, Larry McMurtry and Diana Ossana).
'Blood on the Red Carpet', *Guardian*, 11 March 2006.

Interviews and profiles

Bolick, Katie, 'Imagination Is Everything', *The Atlantic Monthly*, 12 November 1997.
Cowley, Jason, 'Pioneer Poet of the American Wilderness', *The Times*, 5 June 1997.
Doten, Patti, 'Postcards from the Solitary Life', *Boston Globe*, 26 May 1992.
Edemariam, Aida, 'Home on the Range', *Guardian*, 11 December 2004.
Gerrard, Nicci, 'The Inimitable Annie Proulx', *Observer*, 13 June 1999.
Rimer, Sara, 'At Home With: E. Annie Proulx; At Midlife, a Novelist is Born', *The New York Times*, 23 June 1994.
Viner, Katharine, 'Death of the Author', *Guardian*, 6 June 1997.
Wynne-Jones, Ros, 'Happier to Write than Love', *Independent on Sunday*, 1 June 1997.

Reviews: *Postcards*

Bradley, David, 'A Family Running on Empty', *The New York Times*, 22 March 1992.
Bray, Rosemary, 'The Reader Writes Most of the Story', *The New York Times*, 22 March 1992.

Busch, Frederick, 'A Desperate Perceptiveness', *Chicago Tribune*, 12 January 1992.

Durant, Sabine, 'On the Run and Wish You Were Here', *Independent*, 27 March 1993.

Fein, Esther, 'Shutout Ends: It's Men 12, Women 1', *The New York Times*, 21 April 1993.

Leader, Zachery, 'Beyond the Farm', *The Times Literary Supplement*, 15 March 1993.

Mackay, Shena, 'Ode to Billy's Ghost', *Independent on Sunday*, 7 March 1993.

Miller, Lucasta, 'The great American Murderer', *Sunday Telegraph*, 7 March 1993.

Porter, Henry, 'Back off, Ease up, Enjoy', *Guardian*, 6 April 1995.

Shone, Tom, 'Return to Sender', *The Sunday Times*, 28 February 1993.

Streitfield, David, 'PEN picks Woman', *Washington Post*, 21 April 1993.

Walton, James, 'Rooting for a heroic failure', *Daily Telegraph*, 6 November 1993.

Reviews: *Brokeback Mountain*

Atkins, Lucy, 'Review of *Brokeback Mountain*', *The Times Literary Supplement*, 23 October 1998.

Caldwell, Gail, 'Wild West Transplanted to Wyoming', *Boston Sunday Globe*, 16 May 1999.

Eaves, Will, 'Torn up Inside', *The Times Literary Supplement*, 11 June 1999.

Eder, Richard, 'Don't Fence me in', *The New York Times*, 23 May 1999.

Flanagan, Mary, 'Rough and Redneck', *Independent*, 19 June 1999.

Lehmann-Haupt, Christopher, '"Close Range:" Lechery and Loneliness out West', *The New York Times*, 12 May 1999.

Messud, Clare, 'Doomed to Walk the Hard Earth of Wyoming', *Guardian*, 5 June 1999.

Roberts, Michele, 'Sweat and Cheap Soap', *Independent on Sunday*, 6 June 1999.

Showalter, Elaine, 'Annie Proulx', *City Pages*, 22 December 1999.

Skow, John, 'On Strange Ground', *Time Magazine*, 17 May 1999.

Thomson, David, 'The Lone Ranger', *Independent on Sunday*, 30 May 1999.

Thorpe, Vanessa, 'Ranch Hands get Raunchy', *Independent on Sunday*, 2 August 1998.

Brokeback Mountain film reviews

Cohen, Sandy, 'The Story behind *Brokeback Mountain*', *Associated Press*, 19 December 2005.

French, Philip, '*Brokeback Mountain*', *Observer*, 8 January 2006.

Holden, Stephen, 'Riding the High Country, Finding and Losing Love', *The New York Times*, 9 December 2005.

Moody, Rick, 'Across the Great Divide', *Guardian*, 17 December 2005.

Book-length studies of Proulx's work

Patterson, Eric, *On* Brokeback Mountain: *Meditations about Masculinity, Fear, and Love in the Story and the Film*, Lanham, Maryland; Plymouth, UK: Lexington Books, 2008.

Rood, Karen, *Understanding Annie Proulx*, Columbia, South Carolina: University of South Carolina Press, 2001.

Stacy, Jim, *Reading* Brokeback Mountain: *Essays on the Story and the Film*, Jefferson, North Carolina, and London: McFarland and Company, 2007.

Varvogli's, Aliki, The Shipping News: *A Reader's Guide*, New York, London: Continuum, 2002.

Book reviews general

Abell, Stephen, 'Woebegone in Wyoming', *The Times Literary Supplement*, 12 September 2008.

Caveney, Graham, 'That Old Ace in the Hole', *Independent*, 4 January 2003.

Gautreaux, Tim, 'Behind Great Stories there are Great Sentences', *Boston Globe*, 19 October 1997.

Harrison, John, 'A Lot of Bad Geography', *The Times Literary Supplement*, 3 December 2004.

Kendrick, Walter, 'The Song of the Squeeze-Box', *The New York Times*, 23 June 1996.

McCrum, Robert, 'The End of Literary Fiction', *Observer*, 5 August 2001.

Miller, Laura, 'The News from Woolybucket', *The New York Times*, 15 December 2002.

Moore, Caroline, 'That Old Ace in the Hole', *The Spectator*, 4 January 2003.

Myers, B. R., 'A Reader's Manifesto: An Attack on the Growing

Pretentiousness of American Literary Prose', *The Atlantic Monthly*, July/
August 2001.

Oates, Joyce Carol, 'In Rough Country', *The New York Review of Books*, 23
October 2008.

Patterson, Christina, 'Welcome to America', *Observer*, 20 October 1996.

Rafferty, Terence, '"Bad Dirt": A Town with Three Bars', *The New York
Times*, 5 December 2004.

Reynolds, Susan Salter, 'Annie Proulx No Longer at Home on the Range',
Los Angeles Times, 18 October 2008.

Valdes, Marcela, 'Rough Weather', *Washington Post*, 28 September 2008.

Yardley, Jonathan, 'The Naked and the Bad', *Washington Post*, 2 July 2001.

Other useful works

Atwood, Margaret, *Survival: A Thematic Guide to Canadian Literature*, Tor-
onto: Anansi, 1972.

Bradbury, Malcolm, *The Modern American Novel*, Oxford: Oxford University
Press, 1992.

Fiedler, Leslie, *Love and Death in the American Novel*, New York: Criterion
Books, 1960.

Millard, Kenneth, *Contemporary American Fiction: An Introduction to American
Fiction since 1970*, Oxford: Oxford University Press, 2000.

Web links

Proulx discusses the story and film of *Brokeback Mountain* (particularly her
passion for accuracy) in an excellent podcast of *Bookworm – Literature and
Drama* (KCRW) with Michael Silverblatt on 19 January 2006. Available
from: www.podcastdirectory.com/podshows/256265.

Proulx tells the story behind *Brokeback Mountain* at: www.advocate.com/
news_detail_ektid23486.asp.

Proulx's Oscar outburst is available at: www.guardian.co.uk/books/2006/
mar/11/awardsandprizes.oscars2006.

A recent interview with Susan Salter Reynolds of the *Los Angeles Times* (8

October 2008) is of interest, particularly as it shows the writer coming to terms with the legacy of *Brokeback Mountain*:
www.latimes.com/news/nationworld/nation.la-et-proulx18-2008oct18,0,33 83917.story.

Katie Bolick's insightful interview with Proulx for *The Atlantic Monthly* (12 November 1997) is available at: www.theatlantic.com/unbound/factfict/ eapint.htm.

A very good overview of Proulx's life, works, awards, criticism and related links – including the Myers' 'A Reader's Manifesto' is available at: www.answers.com/topic/annie-proulx.